Professional Development
Lifelong Learning Sector

Mentoring

Second Edition

● Susan Wallace and Jonathan Gravells

LearningMatters

First published in 2005 by Learning Matters Ltd.
Reprinted in 2006
Second edition published in 2007

British Library Cataloguing in Publication Data
A CIP record for this book is available from the British Library.

ISBN: 978 1 84445 102 9

The right of Susan Wallace and Jonathan Gravells to be identified as authors of this work has been asserted by them in accordance with the Copyright, Design and Patents Act 1998

Cover design by Topics – The Creative Partnership
Project Management by Deer Park Productions, Tavistock, Devon
Typeset by Pantek Arts Ltd, Maidstone, Kent
Printed and bound in Great Britain by Bell and Bain Ltd., Glasgow

Learning Matters Ltd
33 Southernhay East
Exeter EX1 1NX
Tel: 01392 215560
info@learningmatters.co.uk
www.learningmatters.co.uk

Contents

Introduction

Imagine this. A newly appointed teacher arrives for his first day at work in a big Further Education (FE) college. It's his first job. He doesn't know where the photocopying paper's kept. He doesn't know what pleases the head of department or what makes her irritated. He doesn't know how to find out about his timetable. In fact, he feels as though he doesn't know anything. In the same department there's a teacher of many years' experience. This term she's been asked to teach a group of 14–16 year olds. She's heard they may be unruly, and she's never taught this age group before. The head of department herself is a very recent appointment. She suspects she's been promoted on the strength of her excellent organisational and classroom skills; but she's only ever led smallish teams and has no prior experience of running a department. Like the newly appointed teacher and the colleague facing the challenge of an unfamiliar age group, she is as yet unsure of her strengths and weaknesses in relation to the task ahead of her. And this morning she will be welcoming into the department a very nervous mature student teacher from the local university who is entirely new to teaching and to FE, and is joining the team for a three-week teaching practice.

All of these people are competent and enthusiastic professionals whom it would be a pleasure to work alongside. And what is the one thing that would boost the confidence of each of them, relieve their anxiety and improve their performance on this rather stressful day? Why, of course, being taken under the wing of an effective and appropriately skilled mentor!

This book is about mentoring in the Lifelong Learning sector, and in particular in colleges of Further Education. It sets out to do three things:

- provide practical guidance in the skills needed for successful mentoring;
- examine how a system of mentoring can be successfully implemented, monitored and evaluated within a college or other lifelong learning organisation;
- explore what the 'experts' and theorists have to say about mentoring, and see how well this fits with the reality of day-to-day FE experience.

In so doing, this book makes maximum use of case studies and real-life scenarios. The 'real life' scenarios are, of course, all fictional. Nevertheless, most of them will be immediately recognisable, in one guise or another, to those of us who work, or have worked, in a college of Further Education. This is important. In looking at theory – which we shall also do – we must never lose sight of the day-to-day reality, the context in which such theory will be applied. The test of a good theory is that it works in practice. We read it with a sense of familiarity because we recognise it as something we already do, or have seen done. Or, if it's new to us, we try it out and – bingo – it works! And because this book is addressed largely to practitioners, you will find that it repeatedly tries out mentoring theory by applying it to a realistic FE context.

It is important to stress at the outset, however, that not only does mentoring take several different guises within FE colleges, but also that some relationships or arrangements in FE colleges which are currently referred to loosely as 'mentoring' would not be recognised as such by the world of industry and commerce, which tends on the whole to attach to the term mentor a very specialised and specific meaning. For example, a 'mentor' whose role is simply to assess and comment on a colleague's standard of teaching is, strictly speaking, an assessor or a coach; and may be referred to as such in organisations outside FE. This question of definitions will be explored thoroughly in Chapter One.

In the meantime, we have just said that mentoring in FE takes several different guises. Let's have a look now at what is meant by that.

- The mentor as a resource for a teacher education programme.
- The mentor as an Advanced Skills teacher.
- The mentor as an in-house resource for staff development (particularly in leadership and management).
- The unofficial mentor.

The mentor as a resource for a teacher education programme

Most programmes of teacher education designed specifically for FE, whether in-service (part-time) or pre-service (full-time), and whether provided in-house by the college itself or by a nearby university or Higher Education Institution (HEI) will involve a system of mentoring. This usually means drawing on the time and expertise of experienced and successful teachers by pairing them with a 'student' or 'trainee' teacher to whom they will provide support and guidance – not only in the practicalities of teaching but usually also in a specific subject area – for the duration of the teacher education programme. This role very often involves some element of assessment, particularly of practical teaching; and the terms under which such mentors operate can differ widely from institution to institution. Under some schemes mentors can receive a token payment or be given some hours' remission from their teaching load, while under others they may be expected to operate on the basis of goodwill and as an aid to their own professional development.

The role of mentoring in teacher education programmes is very much the subject of scrutiny at present, and has been so since *Success for All* (DfES, 2002) put teacher education in FE high on the DfES agenda. Ofsted, in its survey of teacher education provision for the FE sector (Ofsted, 2003) has focused on the quality and purpose of mentoring in this context. Its recommendations in relation to mentoring include that:

- greater standardisation is necessary in the quality of mentoring received by student teachers;
- greater emphasis and clearer structure should be given to providing support for the student teacher's subject knowledge.

The first of these issues is a crucial one, and one which, with all the will in the world, is unlikely ever to be resolved completely. There's no doubt that the quality of experience for those on the receiving end of mentoring in such programmes is variable. Imagine the rather vulnerable and not very confident student teacher allocated a mentor who is an excellent role model as far as teaching goes, and highly organised in offering time for discussion of the student teacher's progress, but who is also rather reserved and unapproachable. Despite the admirable qualities of the mentor, what this student teacher may respond to best at this stage is support that falls into the 'warm and fuzzy' category; a mentor whose strengths lie in confidence-building, listening and problem-solving, rather than in superlative classroom practice and good time-keeping. Another student teacher on the same programme, having been given a mentor who is approachable, caring, but slightly disorganised, may find themselves longing for a mentor like the first we described. Now imagine that the Certificate in Education (Cert Ed) programme leader organises an exchange of mentors in order to meet the individual needs of these two student teachers. Their subjective experiences of being mentored will not be uniform, either before or after the exchange. Rather than standardisation, what hopefully has been achieved is a meeting of individuals' needs through a careful matching of those needs with what individual mentors have to offer. Mentoring in any context is a *relationship*, and therefore subject to all the variable human strengths and frailties that impact on relationships of every kind. It's highly doubtful in any case, therefore, that the experience of being mentored on teacher education programmes will ever be entirely standardised – certainly not as long as it involves the human factor.

The *role* of the mentor, on the other hand, may be clearly set out (as we have seen from the above example) and monitored. This offers a way to standardise the *function and responsibilities* of the mentor in FE teacher training, though obviously not the *quality of the relationship*.

The Ofsted recommendation that there should be more structured support of student teachers' subject knowledge may also impact heavily on the role of mentor. Traditionally, a central function of the mentoring system in FE teacher education programmes has been just this: to develop, consolidate and extend the student teacher's knowledge of their specialist subject and to help them to adapt and structure that body of knowledge in an appropriate way so as to meet the learning needs of their students. The reason that this function is so crucial is that the tutors, staff developers and teacher educators on FE teacher education programmes have traditionally focused on the generic skills of teaching and supporting learning. The very nature of the Lifelong Learning sector and FE colleges in particular means that the curriculum encompasses so diverse a range of subjects, both vocational and academic, that it would be an impossibility for professional development or teacher education teams to encompass all these areas of expertise. This means, in effect, that a mentor's contribution to such programmes will be two-fold:

- to model good classroom practice;
- to support the student teacher's grasp of subject knowledge in terms of currency, breadth and appropriate structure for presentation to learners.

Very often, this role is extended to include an element of assessment which may contribute to the overall assessment of the student teacher's performance on the programme. The responsibilities of the mentor may therefore be further expanded to look like this:

- to model good classroom practice;
- to contribute to the assessment of the student teacher's classroom practice;
- to support the student teacher's grasp of subject knowledge in terms of currency, breadth and appropriate structure for presentation to learners;
- to assess the student teacher's grasp of subject knowledge in terms of currency, breadth and appropriate structure for presentation to learners.

Set out in this way, it is clear that the responsibilities of the mentor on award-bearing teacher education programmes are extensive, making the mentor's role a key element in the successful operation of such a programme. And, of course, the current requirement that FE teachers should possess or be working towards a nationally recognised teaching qualification means that, more than ever before, mentoring skills are of crucial importance to the FE sector.

The mentor as an Advanced Skills teacher

A more recent development in FE mentoring has been the creation of the Advanced Skills teacher. The Advanced Skills teacher is often called upon to step into the role of mentor, as described in the last section, for teacher education programmes leading to Stage 2, Cert Ed or Post Graduate Certificate of Education (PGCE) qualifications; but they are also increasingly used outside these formal programmes to support the professional development of individuals in one or more aspects of their professional practice. The role of Advanced Skills teacher has developed alongside other initiatives in FE, such as college self-assessment and structured programmes of appraisal. Such a teacher, who has demonstrated a level of excellence in their own professional practice, is recognised as a valuable resource, in that they are able not only to act as a model of good practice for colleagues who may be less experienced with certain groups, subjects, or behaviours; but also because they can, in some instances, fulfil an assessment role by helping to grade classroom performance in a college's self-assessment exercise. The current importance of self-assessment for colleges means, once again, that the mentor as Advanced Skills teacher has an increasingly important role to play in the Quality Assurance procedures of the college.

As well as offering support and advice to newly appointed colleagues, the Advanced Skills teacher may sometimes find themselves acting as mentor to colleagues who have greater length of experience than themselves, or hold more senior positions. You will find that the skills necessary for handling such situations sensitively, and the ethical issues involved, are among the topics covered in the chapters that follow.

The mentor as an in-house resource for staff development (particularly in leadership and management)

As we have seen, the mentor on teacher education programmes and the Advanced Skills teacher could be (and often are) the same person. The skills they are helping to develop are the skills of teaching and supporting learning as set out in the national standards. Their area of expertise and focus of operation is centred on professional practice in the classroom. However, another set of skills essential to FE are those of leadership and management; and for these, too, there is a set of national standards. Professionals in FE who are newly appointed to leadership and management roles, or who have occupied those roles for some time and are now encountering rapid change in the Lifelong Learning sector, may well benefit from the support of an appropriately skilled and experienced mentor. Except in the case of support for very senior roles, the mentor is likely to be chosen from among suitably qualified colleagues in the same institution. In this mentoring relationship there is less likely to be an element of assessment, the emphasis being firmly upon professional and personal development.

The unofficial mentor

And then there's the unofficial mentor. I guess if we think back most of us have had one or more of those. They are the colleague you instinctively turn to when you want to find out how something is done, or when a session has gone badly and you want a bit of advice, or when you're not sure what mark to award, or even how to get the toner into the photocopier. Or it may go deeper than this. They may be someone whose classroom style you have admired and ever afterwards tried to emulate; or someone who has consistently provided a listening ear while you reflect on your strengths and weaknesses, and has asked just the right questions at just the right time. If you've been in the business for any length of time then it's likely that you yourself have filled this role for various colleagues from time to time. Because mentoring describes a relationship as well as a function, we see aspects of it operating all the time within our working environment, even though it may not be formally named as such.

Outside FE in the wider world of professional development and training, however, as mentioned at the outset, mentor and mentoring are terms used to denote a very specifically defined role and function, around which has developed a body of theory and academic argument which is both interesting and extremely useful to those of us working in and with FE. One of the purposes of this book is to highlight such theory and demonstrate how it may helpfully be applied in order to further improve the quality and effectiveness of mentoring in the context of FE.

Current issues

Most of the literature on mentoring in FE is to be found in the form of articles in academic journals. Normally based on research within colleges, such papers provide useful insight into what are considered to be the key and current issues and debates about mentoring in the FE sector. For example, Woodd (2001) argues that mentoring, in terms of what that role entails, may be understood quite differently by different mentors; and that fundamental skills, such as communication skills, are probably possessed to different degrees by mentors from different subject specialist backgrounds. Hankey (2004) explores what is meant by 'effective' mentoring for teachers' professional development, and particularly the role of reflection in the mentoring process. She also identifies as an issue the difficulties that can arise in finding appropriate subject specialist mentors to support trainee teachers in a sector where curriculum boundaries are not as clear-cut as in schools. Cunningham (2004) raises and addresses the issue of the recruitment and selection of mentors, exploring the possibility of a link between the origins of their involvement (coerced or volunteered) and their subsequent performance as mentors; and concluding that most mentors in the sample, however recruited, found the role rewarding. All these current issues, and more, are addressed in the chapters that follow, and full references to the sample of articles mentioned here can be found at the end of this Introduction.

How to use this book

In this Introduction we have enumerated the types of mentoring usually encountered in colleges of FE and looked at why the issue of mentoring is becoming increasingly important within the sector. We have also highlighted some of the issues that practitioners in FE are identifying as central to mentoring at the present time. In the chapters that follow we shall be looking in detail at what makes for good mentoring (and what doesn't!). This will involve not only a consideration of the practical skills required, but also of how these skills link to the more familiar ones of teaching and supporting learning. If you take a look at the national occupational standards for Teaching and Supporting Learning in the Lifelong Learning sector, and you substitute the word 'mentee' for 'learner' in each case, you'll see that there is a shared ground of expertise between the effective mentor and the effective teacher. If, in addition, you would find it useful to think about your mentoring role in terms of how it can contribute towards your meeting the occupational standards for Leadership and Management in the Lifelong Learning sector, you can find the appropriate guidance in our recent book, Professional Development in the Lifelong Learning Sector: *Leadership and Leading Teams* (Learning Matters, 2007).

In Chapter One we start by defining our terms. What do we mean by mentoring, and what makes it different from similar activities such as coaching, teaching, counselling, or simply 'taking care'? To explore this, we look at a number of mentoring models and theories, and show how these can be helpful when applied to the FE context. In Chapter Two we look at the qualities and attitudes which make for effective mentoring, and we focus on the practicalities of what makes a mentoring relationship work. This chapter also focuses on what qualities and behaviour a mentee can bring to the relationship in order to help it work effectively. Chapters Three and Four concentrate on the practical skills which a good mentor needs, and how these may be developed. We move from essential, first level skills in Chapter Three, such as questioning and summarising, to the more complex skills in Chapter Four, such as challenging and reframing. These two chapters look at ways to get the most benefit from the mentoring relationship and how to avoid the most common pitfalls. New mentors may find these particularly interesting chapters to read, as they include the accounts of several FE professionals who have instructive stories to tell of their own experiences of being mentored.

In Chapter Five we look at the role of coaching within a mentoring relationship, and, in particular, we focus closely on the skills (and art) involved in giving effective feedback – a key facet of the mentor's role. In Chapter Six we explore the importance of reflection and how reflective practice can enhance the mentor's performance as well as the mentor–mentee relationship. Chapter Seven looks at more formal ways of evaluating the effectiveness of mentoring, both on an individual and an institutional level. It explores the question of why we need to evaluate the mentoring process, and gives some practical consideration to how this can be best achieved. We make a link in this chapter between the development of mentoring skills and the development of skills for teaching and supporting learning; and the relationship between both of these and the development of the college as a Learning Organisation. Finally, in Chapter Eight, we bring all these issues together and look at mentoring from an institutional perspective. This chapter looks at the how and why and what of implementing a college-wide mentoring scheme, including the training and development of mentors, and will be of particular interest to those with cross-college responsibility for the setting up, running and monitoring of such initiatives.

This book is structured in such a way that you can choose to read it through, following the arguments from chapter to chapter, or take the chapters in a non-sequential order best suited to your own professional needs. At the end of each chapter you'll find full references to all works cited and, in some cases, suggestions for further reading. We have included references to websites where we think these will be helpful.

Finally it remains to say that we hope you enjoy reading this book as much as we have enjoyed writing it. Happy mentoring!

References

Cunningham, B (2004) Some have mentoring thrust upon them: the element of choice in mentoring in a PCET environment. *Research in Post-Compulsory Education*, 9, 2, pp 271–282.

Department for Education and Skills (2002) *Success for All*. London: DfES.

Hankey, J (2004) The good, the bad and other considerations: reflections on mentoring trainee teachers in post-compulsory education. *Research in Post-Compulsory Education*, 9, 3, pp 389–400.

Office for Standards in Education (2003) *The Initial Training of Further Education Teachers: a survey*. London: HMSO.

Wallace, S and Gravells, J (2007) Professional Development in the Lifelong Learning Sector: *Leadership and Leading Teams*. Exeter: Learning Matters.

Woodd, M (2001) Learning to leap from a peer: a research study on mentoring in a further and higher education institution, *Research in Post-Compulsory Education*, 6, 1, pp 97–104.

www.emccouncil.org.uk (The European Mentoring and Coaching Council website).

1. Definitions

CHAPTER OBJECTIVES

This chapter is designed to help you to:

- develop a clear understanding of how and why we use the term 'mentoring';

- identify some useful distinctions between the role of mentor and the role of coach, teacher, care taker or counsellor;

- recognise and analyse some key mentoring models and theories of mentoring;

- explore ways in which these can be applied to the realities of mentoring in a Further Education college or similar organisation in the Lifelong Learning sector.

Introduction

Most of us, at one time or another, will have experienced the benefits of mentoring or been a mentor ourselves. Many will have done both. We may not have called it mentoring or even recognised the process. Nevertheless it will, like as not, have happened to us.

Our mentor may have come in the guise of a fondly remembered teacher, an older brother or sister, a helpful boss or more experienced work colleague, an apprentice training instructor, or just a close and trusted friend. The chances are it was not part of an organised scheme or even an intentional process. We probably just fell into it in conversation, recognising at some point that here was a person who was helping us to see through our problems, helping us to grow and develop, feel good about ourselves.

Who was Mentor and what does that have to do with FE?

In this respect, mentoring is nothing new. The prototype of this trusted friend and guardian appears in Homer's *Odyssey*. An old friend of Odysseus, called Mentor, agrees to look after his son, Telemachus, whilst the king is away at the Trojan Wars and then battling against the odds to make his way home again. Of course, this being Greek mythology, Mentor is sometimes Athena, the goddess of wisdom, in disguise, providing a field day for commentators fond of the extended analogy. What is the significance of wisdom in mentoring? Should mentors combine the best of male and female characteristics (psychologically rather than physically, one assumes)? How much of their true selves should mentors reveal? You cannot help but feel there must also be a joke in here about wisdom being well-disguised inside some doddery old codger who knows your dad.

Of course, the story of Mentor also raises the question of what we call the person being mentored. Strictly speaking, I suppose it should be 'telemachuses', or maybe 'telemachi', but for some reason this name has never quite caught on, so we are left with 'mentee', which sounds like a new brand of mouthwash. Sadly, no one has been able to come up with anything better, despite an as yet unclaimed reward from the European Mentoring and Coaching Council for doing just that. (If you're feeling inspired, you'll find the website address at the end of this chapter.)

We can all come up with examples, real and fictional, of other mentoring relationships: Merlin and Arthur, Obi Wan Kenobi and Luke Skywalker, Rita and Frank (from *Educating Rita*), even Nelson Mandela and Naomi Campbell apparently. Oh, and every grizzled older cop with a fresh-faced younger colleague in every buddy detective movie you've ever seen.

Distinctions between mentoring, coaching and teaching

So what marks out these relationships as different from being a teacher or a coach or just a friend?

Is it about being older and wiser? But this is generally true of teachers and coaches as well, though not always, particularly in adult education. Equally, whilst it often appears to characterise famous mentors, such as Obi Wan and those others mentioned above, the truth is mentors do not necessarily have to be older and wiser. In fact, one could argue that superior expertise is often less relevant in mentoring than *different* expertise. (Nelson Mandela probably doesn't know much about fashion modelling, but has a wisdom and life experience which one can imagine is inspiring to tap into.) Coaches often have a technical grasp of their field, but don't have to be better performers than those they are coaching (think of coaching top-class athletes). Teachers, on the other hand, are generally expected to be more knowledgeable than their students.

So could the factor which distinguishes mentoring from coaching or teaching be something about the length of the relationship? It is true that mentoring partnerships can last for years, and mentoring is usually a longer term, more gradual process than coaching. But many teaching relationships last a number of years (sometimes to the chagrin of both parties), and occasionally mentoring fulfils its purpose in relatively few meetings.

Perhaps it's that the mentoring relationship is perceived as less directive, focused more on helping people find their own answers? Again there is an element of truth in this and, as we shall see later, ownership of the agenda should generally be more firmly in the hands of the mentee than is the case with students or coachees. (Yes, there is a reward still open to improve that name too.) However, the practice of Socratic dialogue, helping the learner to unearth and articulate their own knowledge or ideas through skilful questioning, is a technique used as much in teaching as in mentoring; and this or similar non-directive methods can sometimes be used in coaching too.

Of course questioning, in a teaching context, does have its limitations, as you are probably beginning to feel right now. If the factor that distinguishes mentoring from coaching or teaching is neither greater age and/or wisdom, nor length of time involved, nor the use of non-directive guidance and support – then what, for pity's sake, is it?

It is, of course, something that encompasses all of these things and more.

TASK

Read the following account, given by an Advanced Skills practitioner, of her experience mentoring a newly appointed teacher, and make a note of the various functions she undertakes within that role as mentor.

I was a bit worried at first about taking Malcolm on as a mentee. When they asked me to do it I thought, 'Wait a minute. He's older than me. He's coming in at the same level as me. He might be new to this place, but he's been at this sort of work years longer than I have. How's he going to feel about being mentored by me?' But it's been fine – better than fine. In fact, it's been really good and I've learned a lot. What did it involve? Well, the first thing, really, was to make sure he knew his way around the place, that he had his intranet password, that he knew who everybody was – all that sort of thing. He hadn't taught any 14–16 year-olds before, so, as well as inviting him to watch me, I sat in on his classes a few times and made some suggestions afterwards about things he might try to keep them interested – things that work for me. And the nice thing was that when we had our regular weekly meetings we got to talk about our subject area as well – social policy stuff – because it turns out we're both interested in that area; and we've passed on email contacts to each other and conference details and stuff like that. But the most rewarding aspect of this mentoring experience – for me – has been the fact that Malcolm has made use of our regular meetings to talk through aspects of his work here that have been particularly difficult for him. It's not that I've been handing out advice all the time or anything like that; it's been more about listening, and maybe asking questions from time to time hopefully to help him clarify things for himself. And Malcolm says he's found that really useful. And it's nice to feel you've been useful, isn't it?

DISCUSSION

In reading that through you've probably noted down at least four functions that Malcolm's mentor is serving; or – to put it another way – four distinct aspects to the mentoring role. They may be summarised as:

- coaching – *sat in on his classes a few times and made some suggestions afterwards*;
- care taking – *make sure he knew his way around the place*;

- networking – *passed on email contacts to each other and conference details and stuff like that*;
- counselling – *listening, and maybe asking questions from time to time hopefully to help him clarify things for himself.*

You may also have noticed that the mentor herself feels that she, too, is gaining professionally from the relationship with the mentee; and we shall be exploring this particular issue in detail later.

Mentoring models

Now, though, let's draw a diagram to help us analyse the relationship between the kinds of help and support which Malcolm's mentor is providing:

Some ways in which mentors give support
(Adapted from Clutterbuck, 1985)

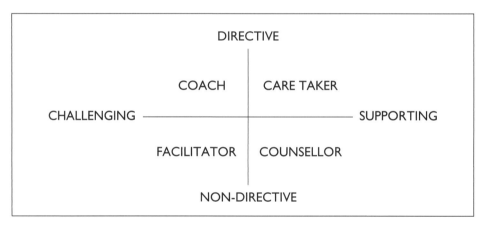

How does this diagram work? Helping relationships can vary in how *directive* they are (how much the helper tries to influence the outcome) and whether they are intended to challenge the person, in terms of learning and development, or support them at a more emotional level. *Coaching* generally has a clear developmental agenda, and seeks to achieve certain agreed aims and objectives; so do teaching, instruction and assessment. Helping someone with their emotional needs, without any preconceived idea of the desired outcome, most of us would recognise as *counselling*. In an educational setting, it is more like the pastoral care provided by a school or college. A more directive form of psychological and emotional support may involve the helper offering advice or acting as a role model, taking a younger, less experienced colleague under their wing. This *caring* role is what many people might regard as a common form of mentoring. Finally, we have a less directive form of developmental help than coaching, here called *facilitating*, but which could equally be called networking. As the terms suggest, this could include putting people in touch with others from whom they could learn, but also helping them to generate and weigh up options and arguments, without suggesting any preferred outcome, like a good chairperson would. If we add these functions to the list we drew above it will now look like this:

- coaching – *sat in on his classes a few times and made some suggestions afterwards* – directive; extends professional expertise;
- care taking – *make sure he knew his way around the place* – directive and supportive;
- facilitating – *passed on email contacts to each other and conference details and stuff like that* – non-directive; extends professional expertise;
- counselling – *listening, and maybe asking questions from time to time hopefully to help him clarify things for himself* – non-directive and supportive.

As this model and the list that follows show, part of the difficulty in defining mentoring is that it may be seen as encompassing a variety of other roles, perhaps employed at different stages of the relationship, as appropriate. How directive is the help required and whether it is more about emotional support or intellectual challenge will have a big impact upon the role which the mentor is called upon to play. For example, if Malcolm had been experiencing difficulties settling into his new job and was lacking in confidence, his mentor would very probably have placed more emphasis on her supportive roles of counsellor and care taker. If, on the other hand, he had been entirely new to teaching or had needed updating in his subject area, his mentor would provide the most effective help by placing emphasis on her role as coach and facilitator, extending Malcolm's classroom skills and helping him access current sources of information.

Now let's have a look at a model which unpacks this even further. It has been developed by Klasen and Clutterbuck (2002). (If you would like to read more about this for yourself, you'll find the full reference at the end of this chapter.)

TASK

Look carefully at the diagram which follows. You will see that within each of the broad roles which we have just identified, there is a continuum of styles and techniques which may be effective.

1. Think of the most recent situation in which you were a mentor or a mentee, and identify where this experience would fit in each of the four quadrants of the chart on page 14. (If you have no prior experience of mentoring or being mentored, use the example described by Malcolm's mentor.)

2. What added dimension do we find in this diagram which may help us to analyse the mentor's role?

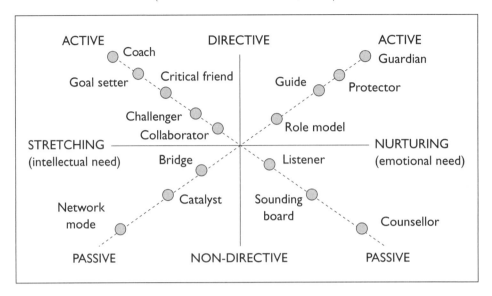

Four basic styles of helping
(Klasen and Clutterbuck, 2002)

DISCUSSION

To answer the first question, let's take Malcolm and his mentor as our example. Judging by the mentor's account, we could probably position her roles on this chart as follows. In terms of counselling she acts as a sounding board, listening as Malcolm articulates his ideas, and prompting him with helpful questions. In terms of networking she is gaining as much as she gives, entering wholeheartedly into network mode. In terms of care taking she acts as guide; and in terms of coaching she seems to be right out there as coach and goal setter. Where she places herself along each of these continua is dictated by the needs of her mentee. If she was mentoring someone other than Malcolm – someone with very different professional development needs – she would, being a responsive mentor, adapt her style accordingly.

The answer to the second question, of course, is that the added dimension in this diagram is provided by the two diagonals, which indicate the degree to which these aspects of mentoring require from the mentor an active or a passive approach. In other words, the extent to which they are behaving proactively (intervening to set goals for the mentee, for example) or allowing themselves to be accessed as a source of support – a resource – by the mentee (acting as a sounding board in a counselling situation, for example). This model provides a useful way to map what is happening within a mentoring relationship, and we shall return to it in later chapters.

The purpose of mentoring

What these two models we have looked at have shown, then, is that mentoring encompasses elements of coaching and teaching, and, for that matter, counselling. What marks it out as different from all of these, however, is its *purpose*. For mentoring is primarily about transition – about helping someone to move from one stage to another. In FE, therefore, mentoring is about supporting someone through the transition from one stage of professional development to another. We use the term transition because we are talking here about a process of change and development that goes deeper than simply acquiring more knowledge.

Telemachus (remember him?) was helped by Mentor to make the transition from boyhood to manhood; Arthur, with the help of Merlin, changed from Sir Kay's humble squire to King of England; Rita, with the support of her university professor, developed from a bored underachiever to an enthusiastic learner and independent thinker. Even those young cops learn more from their worldly-wise partners than just how to do the job. They learn about how to survive and succeed in a particular environment, how the 'system' works.

CLOSE FOCUS

Mentoring is:

> 'off-line help by one person to another in making significant transitions in knowledge, work or thinking.'
>
> (Megginson and Clutterbuck, 1995)

Thinking about the above definition of mentoring, take some time to consider the following questions.

1. How well does this description fit your own experience, either as a mentor or a mentee, or from your observation of the mentoring process within your institution? (If you have no experience at all of mentoring, consider how well the definition fits the account given by Malcolm's mentor earlier in this chapter.)

2. How would you yourself define mentoring, from your own experience, or from what you have read so far in this chapter, or from both? Make a note of your definition at this stage and see whether it changes as you read through the chapters that follow.

DISCUSSION

The definition in Close Focus above is one that conforms to the European school of thought, which sees mentoring as primarily a process leading to personal development. The tradition in the United States, on the other hand, has been much more in favour of a *sponsorship* model. A typical sponsorship arrangement is when an older, more experienced person actively helps a junior employee successfully to climb the career ladder. Our focus in this book, for obvious reasons, will be on the European model – the one described in the quote above.

In both cases, however, mentoring will have two distinct functions. It will enable the mentee to assimilate knowledge, skills and behaviours which help them to make that all-important transition from one stage of professional development to another. At the same time, it can help the mentee to understand and cope with the emotional and psychological challenges that such transition brings. In other words, taking on one's first management role or one's first class of 14-year-olds is as much about establishing relationships, building one's self-confidence and seeking reassurance, as it is about knowing what to do.

So what happens when we hit the next change, or need to develop further? Must we remain in a constant state of being mentored, like some neurotic stereotype, unable to make a decision without consulting our analyst? The answer is no, because the third and perhaps most crucial function of mentoring is to help someone learn *how* to learn. In other words, the result of good mentoring (like good psychotherapy!) is to make someone more able to solve their own problems, to develop themselves and to handle changes in their life successfully.

Mutual learning

It is this emphasis on transition – helping someone progress from one stage or state to another – which makes mentoring such a hugely rewarding task, because in all transitions there is so much potential for *mutual* learning. In other words, it is not only the mentee who will benefit from the relationship; the mentor, too, will usually have much to gain in terms of professional development. How often have we seen the grizzled old cop having learnt greater tolerance, appreciation of what's really important in his life, and a less cynical take on his job, as a result of his partnership with the young rookie? (Probably more often than is good for our digestion.) In this lies a basic truth. So much so that mentoring schemes have even been designed around it, for example in the pairing of older, more senior (and often white, male) managers with younger employees from ethnic minorities, to help improve an organisation's understanding of diversity issues.

Scared? Don't be. Would-be mentors should not be put off by this daunting array of roles and the idea that they, too, are going to be learning something. Not everyone is required or indeed qualified to serve all these functions, and not all mentors do, at first. Indeed, a healthy knowledge of one's own limitations is key to being a responsible mentor and to learning how to get better at it, as we shall see in Chapter Two. But now, to illustrate what we've said so far, let us look at some examples of mentoring roles, and see if you can categorise them as primarily facilitating, coaching, care taking or counselling.

Task

Read through the following list of professional interactions and decide what mentoring function, in your view, each of them is describing: facilitating, coaching, care taking or counselling.

1. Carol, a student teacher, is in college on a six-week teaching practice placement. On her second day in college she goes to see her mentor, Basia, in tears, convinced that one of her students doesn't like her. Basia listens to Carol's story and asks some careful questions which help Carol to gain a more positive perspective on what has happened and to realise that a lot of her distress stems from the fact that she is still understandably unsure of herself as a teacher and nervous that her teaching practice won't go well. Basia's questions also help Carol to realise that this particular student may not like any teacher very much.

2. During her second week of teaching practice, Carol is observed by Basia as she teaches an AS class. Basia then debriefs her and helps her draw up an action plan, helping her to identify her strengths and generate ideas for how she could do some things even better next time.

3. The following day, Carol asks Basia how she should approach a forthcoming discussion with Keith, a senior member of staff who has offered to take her along to a curriculum conference as part of her 'professional development'. She instinctively feels uneasy about this, but is anxious not to cause offence unwittingly, or damage her prospects of a permanent job. Basia informs Carol that this is an unusual offer, in her experience, and helps Carol think through a number of questions she might want to ask both Keith and her placement supervisor before coming to a decision. She offers to speak to Keith on Carol's behalf, but Carol declines for the time being.

4. During the third week of Carol's placement, Basia sets up a team-teaching session in which Carol and Magda, a more experienced teacher from another college, share the teaching of an AS class. Magda has just completed specialist training in video production, a technology that Carol is anxious to feature in a forthcoming classroom assessment. Carol identifies the examples of good practice that she's seen in Magda's teaching, and as well familiarises herself with the technology and makes a useful contact.

Discussion

To those of us working in or around FE, these are all familiar scenarios. Basia, as mentor, finds herself interacting with Carol in four quite different ways.

1. Counsellor – Carol brings her problems to Basia, who listens and acts as a sounding board.
2. Coach – Basia observes Carol's performance, gives feedback and helps her to set performance goals.

3. Care taker – Carol needs help in responding appropriately to a colleague. She is unfamiliar with the norms of behaviour in this environment and Basia can help her find her way through the maze.

4. Facilitator – Basia facilitates an opportunity to share practice with a colleague whose specialist knowledge may be of use to Carol.

In FE we might most readily recognise number 2 above as the archetypal mentor role. But all four of these interactions, and indeed others, as we have seen, are encompassed by the term mentoring as we normally use it day to day in FE. In this book we are, of course, looking at mentoring in its widest sense.

Why has mentoring become such a hot topic now in FE?

As well as the reasons which are specific to FE and which we discussed in the Introduction to this book, there are a number of other possible explanations for the growing emphasis on mentoring as a means of support for professional development. These include the seemingly increased pace of change, greater uncertainty, and growing social pressure for individual autonomy and empowerment in the workplace. Changes in organisation structures in FE have resulted in flatter hierarchies, with fewer obvious career paths and opportunities for promotion. As a result a new career paradigm – a new way of thinking about our careers – has emerged, founded on employability, rather than security of employment. In other words there is less frequently an expectation now of keeping a job in the same institution for life, but rather a growing emphasis on gaining the skills and qualities which will allow us to move on. Staff development and training sections in FE are coming under increasing pressure to demonstrate added value to the organisation, despite fewer resources in terms of staff and budgets. So the introduction of mentoring could be seen as a way of transferring immediate responsibilities for professional development from the training or staff development functions on to line managers and ultimately to individuals themselves. (If you are interested in exploring this theory further, you may like to refer to Megginson and Clutterbuck, 1995, the full reference for which you'll find at the end of this chapter.)

Mentoring v formal staff development courses

This is not entirely a cost issue. There is some evidence that mentoring can provide more *effective* learning than other traditional alternatives. Short course staff development and training has been shown to be generally poor at transferring knowledge and skills since, according to Klasen and Clutterbuck (2002), over a quarter of the content delivered on short courses like these has been forgotten by the time the trainee leaves the classroom and more than three-quarters forgotten within a month. For anyone involved in FE staff development, this is a pretty scary statistic!

Mentoring, on the other hand, can tap into what has been called *situated learning*. This term describes the process – which we all recognise from our own experience – of learning from insights which are gained randomly and accidentally through our everyday work, as well as through planned experience. This means that mentoring can be more adaptable than formal staff development in capturing the relevance of specific individual experience, and in using the learning cycle in a way which best fits the individual's own learning style. (If you want to read more about situated learning you will find references at the end of this chapter.) Those of you familiar with Honey and Mumford's work (1992) will recognise that formal classroom learning may appeal more to the 'theorist' or 'reflector', but may be less engaging for the 'activist' or 'pragmatist', for whom mentoring may be a far more effective means of professional development. But note, too, that this system of categorisation has come in for criticism recently.

If you have not done so already and would like to assess your own learning style by using Honey and Mumford's questionnaire, you might find it interesting to try this on **www.peterhoney.com**.

Of course, another disadvantage of more traditional training approaches can be that they tend to perpetuate the existing received wisdom, as opposed to encouraging people to 'learn how to learn' and thereby to create potentially new insights. Increasingly, we are all recognising the degree of complexity and ambiguity that teachers, team leaders and managers in FE are being required to handle. No training course can prepare you for this, but mentoring can provide support in developing your *own* strategies for prioritising and reconciling these conflicting demands.

Finally, growing acceptance of the importance of 'soft skills' and emotional intelligence in leadership roles has added to the interest in coaching and mentoring as development approaches. Soft skills and emotional intelligence are about the important skills of relating to others. They are about empathy – the ability to imagine ourselves in someone else's shoes and allow ourselves to gain some insight into what they may be feeling. They are about relating to others with mutual respect rather than, for example, simply as someone with seniority. To learn more about emotional intelligence you may like to refer to Goleman (1996) for which you'll find a full reference at the end of this chapter.

Summary

So why is mentoring particularly valuable as a means of professional development for those of us working in FE? I think one of the answers to this is that mentoring is, as we have already discussed in this chapter, an effective means of drawing out tacit knowledge. By tacit knowledge we mean knowledge we have already gained, but have not yet fully articulated to ourselves, nor reflected on. As adults and professionals we each have our store of tacit knowledge and accumulated wisdom, a result of our experiences of life and work. Encouraging us to access that knowledge and experience, make it explicit, and use it to enhance our professional practice, is one of the prime functions of mentoring. And if that developmental model sounds familiar, it's because it has a lot in common with the principles underlying the way we teach and support learning in the post-compulsory, Lifelong Learning sector.

In the following chapters we shall explore the skills and qualities that make a good mentor, and look at some examples of how mentoring works (and sometimes fails to work!) in practice.

References and further reading

Alred, G, Garvey, B and Smith, R (1998) *The Mentoring Pocketbook*. Alresford, Hants: Management Pocketbooks Ltd.

Clutterbuck, D (1985) *Everyone Needs a Mentor*. London: CIPD.

European Mentoring and Coaching Council website: **www.emccouncil.org.uk**

Goleman, D (1996) *Emotional Intelligence*. London: Bloomsbury.

Honey, P and Mumford, A (1992) *The Manual of Learning Styles*. Third edition, Honey.

Klasen, N and Clutterbuck, D (2002) *Implementing Mentoring Schemes – A Practical Guide to Successful Programs*. Oxford: Butterworth Heinemann.

Lave, J and Wenger, E (1990) *Situated Learning: Legitimate Peripheral Participation*. Cambridge, UK: Cambridge University Press.

Megginson, D and Clutterbuck, D (1995) *Mentoring in Action*. London: Kogan Page.

2. How to be a good mentor and mentee

CHAPTER OBJECTIVES

This chapter is designed to help you to:

- explore some of the qualities and attitudes which are important for effective mentors;

- develop a model for the mentoring process, and consider the importance of reflecting on the relationship itself;

- recognise the importance of sorting out the boundaries of the relationship from the very beginning and the practicalities of how it will work;

- recognise the importance of discussing the mentor's and mentee's expectations, and the need for a continuing dialogue if both parties are really to get the most from the mentoring;

- consider what makes a good mentee;

- identify ways in which the attitude and behaviour of the mentee can have at least as much impact on the success or failure of a mentoring partnership as can the actions of their mentor;

- consider how building self-awareness and reflexivity can help both parties.

Essential qualities and basic processes

A great deal has been written about how to be a good mentor in the context of commercial organisations; but very little, to date, on how to be a good mentor in FE. We shall be looking in this chapter at how some of these general ideas of what makes for effective mentoring can be applied to FE, as well as coming up with a few of our own. But before we look at what others have to say, let's take some time to consider your own views – your own tacit or explicit knowledge.

TASK

What do you think would be the most important attributes of an effective mentor? List the first three or four attributes that come to mind, identifying if you wish the one you consider the most important of all. Then compare what you have written with our list below.

DISCUSSION

It's likely that your list includes one or more of the following.

- A desire to help others develop their potential: sounds soppy maybe, but mentoring may prove too challenging a calling if the mentor ignores its prime purpose.
- A desire to learn and grow continuously yourself: people who feel they know it all, or know as much as they really want to, do not generally make good mentors.
- An open mind which can suspend judgement of others: mentoring works best if you can approach your mentee with what Carl Rogers (1983) called 'unconditional positive regard'. This is tough. We can all think of people who frankly stretch our unconditional positive regard to breaking point and you may end up mentoring one or two of them.
- A wish to give something back: to use your accumulated experience and, dare we say it, wisdom to help the next generation succeed. Research has identified this concept, which you'll sometimes see termed *generativity* as a common motivator for mentors.
- Experience of being mentored yourself: and perhaps a continuing inclination to seek this sort of help. Most mentors enter into the role because they have personally experienced its effectiveness. But, more importantly, a key indication of one's desire to continuously learn and grow is to seek such help yourself. After all, no one trusts a chef who does not eat in their own restaurant.

One of the first things you will notice about this list is that it emphasises qualities, rather than skills. This emphasis on ways of being rather than ways of *doing* – motivation and attitude rather than strategies and competences – has several implications which we are going to explore in the following section.

Ways of being a good mentor

Let's have a look at one teacher's account of being mentored and see what sort of structures or patterns we can identify that we might sum up as ways of mentoring. Read Dina's account through carefully and note down your ideas as you go. You will find this useful when you come to compare your own thoughts and insights with the detailed analysis that follows.

> *I'm lucky because Ivan has been a really good mentor to me. He's never pulled rank or made me feel self-conscious about the gap in our ages and our experience. I watched a couple of his lessons to begin with, and as a teacher he's awesome. So it was scary at first to have him sitting in with me, but he was so nice and relaxed about it that it sort of took the edge off my nervousness. And he was completely open about his own strengths and weaknesses. He'd say stuff like, 'Did you see how I got it wrong with that group? How do you reckon I should have done it?' So I was much more at ease, realising that even he wasn't absolutely perfect.*

> *Anyway, this is how we did it; this is how the mentoring went. We sat down right at the beginning and agreed stuff about confidentiality, and what we would and wouldn't include in our discussions, and when we'd meet and that sort of thing. He was always there. He never cancelled on me, not once. Every week, on Tuesdays, we'd have a meeting for about 40 minutes – take our sandwiches. It worked out well because we were both free at the same time. I don't know how it works for people whose timetables don't work out – and goodness knows you're lucky if you get any free time at all in this business, even to eat. But anyway, we had these meetings and first of all we'd talk about my professional development plan and whatever other work-related stuff was most on my mind, and he'd ask me questions and get me to think it all through. Sometimes he'd suggest things that it would be useful for us to talk about as well – things he'd picked up on from sitting in on my teaching, because he was doing that every couple of weeks or so.*
>
> *It was really useful talking things over with him. It helped me build my confidence up because it made me realise that I can actually talk a lot of sense if I put my mind to it! I learned a lot from that – partly from things Ivan said, but also from things I came up with myself. He helped me see things about myself – strengths mainly, but also things I needed to develop – that I just hadn't been aware of before. And he never hurried me over things. He'd let me drone on sometimes when I was trying to work things out, just letting me think out loud, really. And somehow he managed never to look bored or impatient. And he never made me feel I was being stupid or wasting his time. He made me feel he was really, genuinely interested in how I was doing, and that he really cared about me from the point of view of my professional development.*
>
> *So they felt really useful, those meetings. I always came away feeling I'd gained something, that I understood stuff better. And I never came away without some points for my action plan – professional development plan, we call it. And then the next meeting we'd start again by talking about how I was doing on the PDP – sorry, professional development plan. And that was how it went. It worked great for me. I was really lucky.*

DISCUSSION

Unlike the coaching literature, which is full of acronyms to help practitioners follow a practical process and structure their sessions accordingly, writers on mentoring have been more reluctant to propose such step-by-step guides. This is perhaps because, as we saw in Chapter One, mentoring involves such a mix of roles, including coaching, that it is difficult to be too prescriptive. However, one of the attributes of a good mentor on the list we've just looked at is a thirst for knowledge and a commitment to continuous learning and development. So it's entirely appropriate that we pause to take a look here at what the current literature on mentoring does have to tell us about ways of being a good mentor. First let's compare Dina's account with a recognised depiction of the mentoring process.

This diagram is based on one devised by Alred et al (1998). (If you want to read more of what Alred et al have to say about mentoring, you'll find a reference at the end of this chapter.)

Mentoring process

Let's take each of these stages, look at what they mean in practical terms and see how they compare with Dina's experience of the mentoring process.

Exploration

This model shows us how the process of mentoring generally starts with examining the mentee's current situation in some depth. The aim of this is not simply to ensure that the mentor understands the issues and concerns, but to help the mentee develop a deeper understanding of the topic as well:

> *first of all we'd talk about my professional development plan and whatever other work-related stuff was most on my mind, and he'd ask me questions and get me to think it all through.*

We all have blind spots when we talk about ourselves, things others recognise but we do not. (We shall be looking at this issue of blind spots in more detail in Chapter Four.)

> *He helped me see things about myself – strengths mainly, but also things I needed to develop – that I just hadn't been aware of before.*

As with other kinds of problem-solving, this crucial stage of exploration, of defining the problem, is all too often the one that is rushed or skipped over too lightly. The result is we rush to judgement, solve the wrong problem, or tackle the symptoms and not the causes. This is bad enough if we are fixing the plumbing or mending a faulty circuit, but in mentoring we are dealing with a human being, another person's intellectual, emotional and even spiritual development. It does not always follow a predictable, rational pattern and it is not something one can 'fix'. Reaching snap judgements about what a person's problem is and telling them how to go about sorting it out makes for amusing television comedy but damaging mentoring. Another problem with jumping to conclusions is that what the mentee presents as the issue they would like to address can sometimes hide a related concern which is the real cause of their distress. (Do you remember Carol in Chapter One?)

New understanding

In the second stage of this model the mentor is helping the mentee to seek different perspectives on the issue under discussion. This may require a degree of challenge, carefully applied, to broaden the mentee's perspective and encourage them to look at matters in a different light. The purpose here is to look not just at what has happened but why it has happened:

> *So they felt really useful, those meetings. I always came away feeling I'd gained something, that I understood stuff better.*

It can often be helpful to re-frame issues that we are struggling with, to see them in a different context. This makes us question our long-standing 'mental models' and see potential ways forward that otherwise our preconceptions would have blinded us to. In turn this helps us to generate options, explore 'what ifs' and consider alternative strategies.

One of the most over-used phrases to describe a mentor is 'sounding board', and this is hardly surprising, since a key purpose of mentoring is to create 'personal reflective space' for the mentee. The mentor's job is to help the mentee draw learning from events and think through their own solutions in a questioning but non-judgemental environment:

> ...he'd ask me questions and get me to think it all through...

This is the role of 'critical friend', someone who will question your taken-for-granted assumptions and your unconscious prejudices, but who does so from a genuine desire to see you succeed.

Action planning

Ultimately there can be no change or learning without action, and potential strategies and options must be narrowed down and prioritised into some form of action plan if the process is to move forward:

> And I never came away without some points for my action plan – professional development plan, we call it.

These actions can take many forms. They may be commitments to further investigation or research, a resolve to experiment with a new behaviour or technique, or an agreement to tackle an activity which will unearth new learning by taking the mentee out of their normal comfort zone. No matter how trivial or short term, the commitment to action is important in generating momentum and further opportunities to reflect and learn. This is, after all, no different to the learning cycle with which many of you will already be familiar:

The learning cycle
(Honey and Mumford, 1992)

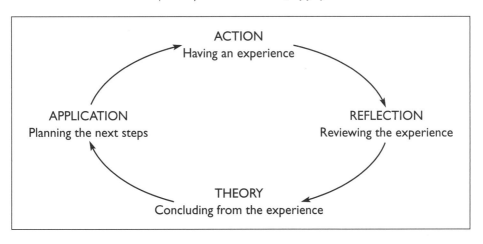

Without planning and action, there is a danger that mentoring becomes a talking shop, a cosy chat, which may feel very therapeutic but which is unlikely to result in much new learning.

Looking at that learning cycle also suggests a way in which we might refine the mentoring model as we have described it so far. What the cycle shows us is that the process is not simply linear, but that in reality it is a cycle. No sooner have we carried out our action plan than we are once again reflecting on what this has taught us. We can see this clearly from looking again at something Dina says at the end of her account:

> And I never came away without some points for my action plan – professional development plan, we call it. And then the next meeting we'd start again by talking about how I was doing on the PDP – sorry, professional development plan.

This means that the mentoring process, if it's working effectively, is not a simple series of steps, but a continuous and multi-layered process. As a mentor you are likely to find yourself working through this cycle in the course of a single meeting, or even in part of a meeting, perhaps having focused on one narrowly defined issue. Equally, of course, you could apply this cyclical model to the entire mentoring relationship, as the mentee develops new understanding and applies their learning accordingly. As the aim of all this is personal development, we should ideally see the process not even as circles but as individual spirals within an overall spiral of learning and growth. Many of us in FE – particularly those of us involved in teacher training and staff development – will already be familiar with this concept in the context of the *spiral curriculum*, where the learner returns to the same issues several times in the course of their professional development, each time gaining an added depth of knowledge and understanding.

Managing the relationship

Is it enough to work our way through any of these models from meeting to meeting, distilling our learning and fulfilling our action plans? Is there not a danger that it could all become a bit mechanistic and self-indulgent? If we believe in continuous learning, then shouldn't we also be learning how to make the mentoring more effective?

To do this we must, as part of what we do, reflect on the process itself and the nature of the relationship. If this all sounds a bit like peering at your own navel then consider this. How many relationships succumb to misunderstanding, atrophy, stagnation or sheer boredom because the parties are so focused on doing stuff that they forget to 'service' the relationship and talk about how it's all going? (Husbands/wives/girlfriends/boyfriends may recognise this line of argument.) Like any one-to-one relationship, mentoring requires us occasionally to step back and look at how it is working, and to treat building and maintaining rapport as pretty much a continuous task. We shall be looking at this in more detail in Chapter Six where we focus on the importance to mentors of reflecting on their practice.

Contracting

Deciding together what our expectations of the relationship are, and agreeing the boundaries as well as the practicalities of how it will work, are often referred to as 'contracting'. This is when we answer such questions as:

- How do we ensure confidentiality?
- Who is responsible for what in the relationship?
- How long do we expect it to last, in the first instance?
- How often will we meet and where?
- How formal do we want it to be?
- How do we decide when it's over?
- What degree of challenge or intimacy are we comfortable with?

You may have noticed from reading Dina's account that she and her mentor addressed these kinds of issues at the very outset:

> *We sat down right at the beginning and agreed stuff about confidentiality, and what we would and wouldn't include in our discussions, and when we'd meet and that sort of thing.*

We might view this as just another part of the exploration stage, but there is a difference. The difference is that contracting focuses on the relationship and the process itself, not on the mentee's particular learning needs. Without the contracting process, the mentoring process can fall into difficulties right from the very start. Look at this account, for example, from Mark, a PGCE FE student on his first teaching practice in a large FE college.

My mentor? I could never find her. And when I did manage to track her down it was always, 'Sorry, Mark. I haven't got time at the moment.' And so it always ended up with me trying to keep up with her while she was striding down the corridor, me trotting along at her elbow trying to ask her pretty important stuff like, 'What do I do if a fight breaks out?' and, 'What happens if half the students turn up late? Do I just start anyway?' And stuff like that. And she's going, 'I'm sorry, Mark. Come and see me later.' But what's the point of that? I'll probably never find her later. And anyway I need to know that stuff now.

Hopefully, not too many people share Mark's experience of being mentored; but he could have been spared this if there had been an initial stage of contracting at which point a regular meeting – however brief – could have been agreed upon, and Mark could have made it clear that in his first few weeks he would probably find a lot of questions he would need the answers to – urgently. At this stage, if it became clear that his mentor was unable or unwilling to allocate sufficient time to the relationship, another mentor might be found and Mark would not be left feeling so totally unsupported.

Of course it's easy to suppose that contracting, like building rapport, is a one-off task. However, in our experience, both must continuously be re-visited in order to ensure that the mentoring relationship is continuing to meet the expectations of both parties, and to avoid it stagnating or, worse, becoming 'toxic'.

The mark 2 mentoring model

(No pun intended.) If we incorporate all of these ideas into our process model we end up with something like this.

Mentoring model

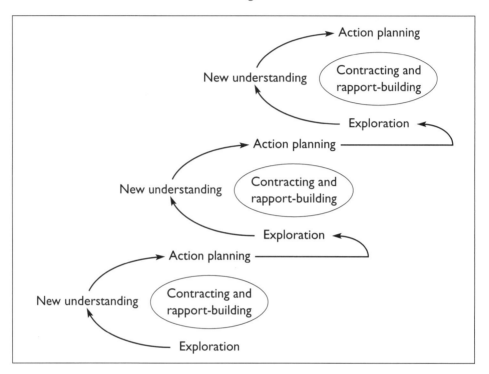

At which point, however, we must issue a couple of health warnings.

- All models are necessarily simplistic and can never convey all the complexities of the learning relationship.
- The best models are those you develop yourself from your own experience, so treat this as no more than a helpful start!

CLOSE FOCUS

Think of a positive mentoring relationship in which you have been involved, formally or informally, either as mentor or mentee. If nothing springs to mind, use the account of mentoring that Dina gives above. Now think about what it is that makes, or made, that relationship work well. Have a go at representing that mentoring process in diagrammatic form. Keep a note of this model. It is likely to be the one you will find most useful when analysing your effectiveness as a mentor or your needs as a mentee.

The good mentee

So far we have said a lot about what makes for a good mentor, but if we believe that responsibility for learning lies squarely with the learner, in adult education at least, then it follows that the mentee must also take some responsibility for the success of the mentoring relationship. In fact, you could argue that this is the premise on which good mentoring is founded. So perhaps we should say more about what makes for a 'good' mentee.

TASK

Murray has been assigned to mentor Stuart, a new lecturer in mechanical engineering. Take a look at this conversation between Stuart and his friend Dave, and identify what less-than-helpful behaviours you think may be driving his mentor to distraction.

Stuart   *Had another meeting with Murray this morning. Really had to dash after he called to remind me. Then, after running all the way over to his office, the first thing he asks is 'What do I want to talk about?'. I mean, how the hell should I know? I thought he was supposed to be helping me.*

Dave   *How's he do that then?*

Stuart   *Well, that's just it. He's my mentor, which kind of means he tells me how to be a good lecturer, but that's what I've spent a year of PGCE doing. I've always got good feedback from all my classroom assessments, so obviously I know how to do the job. What do I want with some old geezer, who learnt how to teach in the dark ages, telling me what to do?*

Dave   *Still, I expect he can give you some tricks of the trade.*

Stuart   *I keep asking to see his lesson plans, so I can copy the best bits, but he keeps ducking the question, asking me to talk about how I plan my stuff. Then when I tell him, he asks about other ways of doing it, but I can't be bothered with that. I've got a good system now. Why the hell should I mess about with it? If it ain't broke, why fix it? That's my motto. He seems to think I'm still in training. Anyway, I can't say I think much of his preparation. He never even seems to have decided what we're supposed to be discussing when we do meet. I felt so sorry for him the last time, that I asked for his help with how to handle Leena, this really quiet lass in one of my classes. Blow me, if he didn't ask me what I thought I should do. I mean he's supposed to be the bloody expert. Why can't he just tell me the answer? It's not 20 questions we're playing here.*

Dave   *So, have you told him you're cheesed off?*

Stuart   *You must be kidding! I made that mistake before, when I was feeling a bit down last term. I tried to explain to Murray that they'd cocked up the timetabling and I'd got behind on marking 'cos so many assignments had come in late. They just don't seem to apply any sanctions here, and the admin staff need a rocket up their backside ... Anyway, I took the opportunity to unload a bit, as I was with him, and he started talking about an action plan, for Pete's sake! I mean, an action plan for me. I'd just spent half an hour telling him who was to blame. Why doesn't he give them an action plan?*

DISCUSSION

There are a number of headings we can use to explore the less constructive aspects of Stuart's behaviour as a mentee. We've given them names to make them easier to remember. Let's see if you came up with some of the same issues as us.

The Scarlet Pimpernel

They seek him here; they seek him there ... Stuart is clearly a difficult man to pin down.

> *Really had to dash after he called to remind me.*

We all have our own ways of managing our time and organising ourselves, and we do not all have to be Filofax freaks or PDA pokers. But sufficient personal organisation to remember and prepare for meetings is essential to making a mentoring relationship work. This is not just a matter of practicality. If someone is taking time out to help you, it is only common courtesy to respect their time enough to show up promptly.

The Jobsworth

Stuart's lack of attention to timekeeping is indicative of another problem. He simply takes no responsibility for the mentoring relationship. As far as he's concerned, it's not his problem to think about what he wants out of it, nor to prepare for meetings.

> *... the first thing he asks is 'what do I want to talk about?'. I mean, how the hell should I know? I thought* he *was supposed to be helping* me.

Stuart expects his mentor, Murray, not just to give up his time and devote it to helping him but to anticipate what his particular learning needs might be (presumably by extra-sensory perception). He is happy then for Murray to plan and run their meeting, with Stuart as a sort of interested observer, just so long as he does not have to do anything. Good mentees take an *active* role in managing the relationship, rather than waiting passively for learning to be 'delivered'.

The Know-it-all

Stuart is confused as to Murray's role, and this is partly because he is protective of his own sense of competence. Whether this is because he is arrogant and over-confident, or actually because he is insecure and covering it with bravado, the result is the same.

> *What do I want with some old geezer, who learnt how to teach in the dark ages telling me what to do?*

Stuart convinces himself he has nothing to learn, and this is the kiss of death to mentoring. A desire to seek feedback and to learn and grow (on the part of both mentor *and* mentee) is a prerequisite of successful mentoring, just as it is of any successful learning relationship.

The Leech

On the few occasions that Stuart admits to wanting a little help, he would prefer to take the line of least resistance. He wants to copy Murray's way of doing things because this requires the least effort and learning on his part (passivity again), and he can easily blame Murray if none of it works.

> *Why can't he just tell me the answer? It's not 20 questions we're playing here.*

In an ideal world Stuart would like to suck Murray dry of a career's worth of learning and save himself the trouble of making sense of his own experience. It will never work of course, because we have to develop our own style which suits our own values, beliefs and personality. Murray is a good enough mentor to recognise that the greatest gift he can give Stuart is not the answers, but the ability to work out his own answers. To do this Murray will have to resist the temptation to hurl Stuart out of a third floor window.

The Victim

Did you notice how nothing ever seems to be Stuart's fault? It sounds as though his greatest contribution to a mentoring meeting was a lengthy whinge about how everyone else was making his life difficult. It is another sign of Stuart's unwillingness to take responsibility for his own performance and learning. The mythical 'they' are always to blame, absolving him of any need to confront what he might actually do to change or improve things.

> *I mean, an action plan for* me. *I'd just spent half an hour telling him who was to blame. Why doesn't he give* them *an action plan?*

Stuart fails to acknowledge that he might want a plan that enables him to keep getting better at what he does. This is, after all, what continuous learning and development is all about. This plan should come largely from him, not be 'given' to him by his mentor.

So how do we spot the 'good mentee'?

- Good mentees take *responsibility* for the success of the mentoring relationship and for their own development needs. They do not search for scapegoats to blame for their own shortcomings. They agree what they want from the mentoring and come to meetings having thought about their own agenda. They take the initiative.
- Good mentees show *respect* for the time and effort being devoted to them by their mentor and keep their appointments (or reschedule in advance). If they feel things are not working, they talk it through with their mentor rather than simply not showing up.
- Good mentees are *responsive* to help. They are open to new ideas and new perspectives. They are committed to change and improvement, and keen to agree actions which will help them learn and develop their skills.

- Good mentees are *reflective*. They want to work out their own answers and their own ways of doing things. They don't want someone else's solutions on a plate. They may even want to challenge the mentor, in the interests of understanding things better. They see mentoring as a way of raising their self-awareness, so they can get better at learning from their own experience.

Summary

In this chapter we have seen how, in order to be a mentor, your motivation and attitude towards the role are every bit as important as the skills which we shall be looking at next.

The same goes for the mentee, who should ideally take responsibility for the relationship, actively seeking help and reflecting on their own personal and professional development.

We have seen how the mentoring process can be thought of as a virtuous spiral, in which aspects of the mentee's development are looked at thoroughly in order to gain different insights, before a commitment to some form of action which will move the mentee to a new level of understanding. This cycle of activity is closely linked to the learning cycle with which you will already be familiar.

In order to get the most out of this process, mentor and mentee should agree boundaries and expectations from the very beginning and revisit this contract on a regular basis. Open discussion about the quality of the relationship will help to build and maintain rapport, as the nature of the relationship and the topics addressed change over time.

References and further reading

Alred, G, Garvey, B and Smith, R (1998) *The Mentoring Pocketbook*. Alresford, Hants: Management Pocketbooks Ltd.
Honey, P and Mumford, A (1992) *The Manual of Learning Styles*. Third edition, Honey.
Rogers, C (1983) *Freedom to Learn for the 80s*. Columbus, OH: Merrill.

3. Mentoring skills 1

Essential mentoring skills

Now that we've explored the qualities that go to make up the 'mentoring mindset', and looked at some of the ways we can characterise the process, let's turn our attention to some of the essential or first level skills required of a good mentor.

These are the skills essential to any meaningful one-to-one dialogue. They can be summarised as:

- building rapport;
- listening;
- questioning;
- reflecting back;
- summarising.

Let's look at each of these in turn, as they apply to mentoring.

Building rapport

In order to create that personal reflective space that we talked about earlier – a questioning but non-judgemental environment in which to help the mentee reflect on and learn from key incidents and think through their own solutions

– there needs to be an openness and sense of ease in the relationship. As a mentee, you need to feel your mentor cares about your development and has your best interests at heart. In other words, you have to trust them.

There is no doubt that personal chemistry plays a large part in the success or otherwise of mentoring relationships, but compatibility is not necessarily about having similar personalities or attitudes. Being mentored by someone with a very different outlook and background from you may initially be more challenging, but can also result in more learning. No relationship will work well, however, if there is no trust.

So, what is it, aside from our natural charm, that helps build this trust? Let's go back to Dina and Ivan – a mentoring relationship that we know has worked well – and look at the elements that have contributed to the building of trust.

TASK

Read through the elements that contribute to the building of trust listed below and then return to Chapter Two and read through Dina's account of being mentored by Ivan again. Can you find examples of these trust-building elements in Ivan and Dina's relationship?

Elements that contribute to the building of trust:

- Maintaining a transparent process.
- Maintaining confidentiality.
- Being honest about ourselves.
- Being patient.
- Doing what you say.
- Not judging.
- Body language and 'matching'.

DISCUSSION

Maintaining a transparent process

Clear and well-aligned expectations of the relationship from the beginning will help to avoid misunderstandings and suspicions about people's motives, so contract carefully.

> *... this is how we did it; this is how the mentoring went. We sat down right at the beginning and agreed stuff about confidentiality, and what we would and wouldn't include in our discussions, and when we'd meet and that sort of thing.*

This is not a one-off exercise, as we have said. Keep revisiting the process. Talk about the relationship regularly and don't be afraid to share models as route maps of where you think you've got to. You may find you are in two different places.

Maintaining confidentiality

After all, as a mentee you are unlikely to be forthright about your strengths, acknowledge your fears and weaknesses, and face up to your blind spots, if you think that your foibles may be posted on the internet the following day.

We sat down right at the beginning and agreed stuff about confidentiality.

Being honest about ourselves

The original Mentor may well have been the goddess of wisdom in disguise, but the chances are you are not, and no one expects you to be. Talking about your own experiences, in moderation and when relevant, may well be helpful, but self-disclosure, talking about your associated feelings (what Egan, 2002, calls 'sharing empathetic highlights') will also inspire trust.

And he was completely open about his own strengths and weaknesses. He'd say stuff like, 'did you see how I got it wrong with that group? How do you reckon I should have done it?' So I was much more at ease, realising that even he wasn't absolutely perfect.

Being patient

Sometimes you have to let people talk, however rambling it may appear to be. Being mentored can be a bit like dreaming (though we suggest you try to stay awake!). It helps us to relive experiences and untangle their real meaning. This is where the learning takes place, and sometimes people have to be allowed to get there on their own.

And he never hurried me over things. He'd let me drone on sometimes when I was trying to work things out, just letting me think out loud, really. And somehow he managed never to look bored or impatient.

Doing what you say

Integrity is vital to building trust and rapport. This goes for respecting meeting arrangements, following up agreed actions, coming back to the mentee when you said you would, etc. Much as you may want to help, do not make grandiose promises that you then cannot deliver on. One broken promise can undo weeks of successful rapport-building.

We sat down right at the beginning and agreed ... when we'd meet and that sort of thing. He was always there. He never cancelled on me, not once.

Not judging

Easy to say, very hard to do, but we all know that we feel more inclined to bare our souls to someone who will not judge us. It's that unconditional positive regard (Rogers, 1983) again. For the mentor it means being sufficiently self-aware of our own prejudices and preconceptions to be able to recognise when they are impinging on the task of helping the mentee.

> And he never made me feel I was being stupid or wasting his time. He made me feel he was really, genuinely interested in how I was doing, and that he really cared about me from the point of view of my professional development.

Body language and 'matching'

Yes, there are aspects of technique which can help in establishing rapport, and certainly open body language, appropriate environment, proper seating arrangements, etc. are more likely to result in a relaxed conversation. However, do not be fooled into thinking this is enough. We can all recognise when we're being 'techniqued' by someone who has just been on the two-day course, and we usually resent it. Trust is about openness, authenticity and the willingness to suspend judgement. Authenticity is not always best served by techniques that may be viewed as manipulation.

From Dina's purely verbal transcript it's of course impossible to pick up issues like body language and seating arrangements. But when you read through Dina's account you will probably have pictured a meeting between her and her mentor. It might be interesting to think about exactly what this picture looked like.

Summary

The above is not an exhaustive list. For instance, the whole of the next section, on listening, contributes massively to rapport-building. What we are striving for is empathy, an over-used and sometimes unhelpful term, unless we talk about how it is demonstrated. All of the actions above, as well as listening with genuine care and interest, will go a long way towards demonstrating empathy and establishing trust. As Ivan clearly did.

Listening

One could argue that listening is the communication skill we use the most, but are taught about the least. It is because we take it for granted that we are often so bad at it. In mentoring, as in any one-to-one interchange, it is not enough just to listen. We have to show we are listening. This is often referred to as 'active listening'.

Active listening is the skill of concentrating on what someone is saying and demonstrating that you have heard and understood what they have said. You may well be aware of this from other training, but here is a reminder of some of the ways we can listen actively.

- Maintain regular eye contact (not continuous eye contact which is just plain scary).
- Try to focus entirely on the other person. Be there for them, and leave your own concerns and distractions outside.
- Do not start thinking of your next question as soon as you've asked the previous one.
- If you must write notes try to keep them brief, or stop the conversation to write them.
- Do not be afraid of silence. Silence can be helpful in slowing down the conversation and allowing reflective space.
- Try to let the other person finish what they are saying without interrupting. (Dialogue is characterised by taking turns. Of course, not everyone seems to recognise this so occasional 'management' of the discussion may be necessary.)
- Watch your body language. Leaning forward and nodding demonstrates interest. Leaning back, folding your arms and looking at the ceiling does not.
- Make encouraging noises (uh-huh...right...yes...I see...tell me more...really?).
- Summarise to help check understanding.

Questioning

A potential subject for a book in its own right, questioning is a crucial skill for mentoring, as it is for teaching. A great training exercise for mentoring is to try to conduct a mentoring session entirely by asking questions. It is an impractical constraint for normal relationships, but a good way of disciplining ourselves into allowing the mentee to discover their own ideas and solutions. Most people find it incredibly hard to do, and that is because most of us, in our desire to help, want to provide a lifeline, an answer to the problem. After all, surely the reason we are mentoring is because we are more experienced and knowledgeable? To make matters worse, mentees will frequently ask for such direct advice. So doesn't that make it right to give it?

Of course the answers to these questions about mentoring are the same as for teaching, particularly for teaching adults. The learning we discover for ourselves is always better remembered, and solutions we find for ourselves are always the ones we are most committed to. Questions play a vital role in this process.

Let's remind ourselves of the main types of question, and where they might best be used.

Open questions

Questions that require more than a simple yes or no answer.

- Tell me about...
- What would you like to discuss?
- How did you feel about...?

These are the questions good mentors use the most, because they are ideal for exploring issues and getting information, for helping people to open up.

Probe questions

Questions that follow up a topic in more detail.

- What do you mean when you say...?
- Tell me a bit more about...?
- How do you know...?

Again used extensively in exploration, these questions ensure that the relevant issues have been fully examined and assumptions have not been taken for granted.

Hypothetical questions

Questions which open the mind to new possibilities.

- What if you were to...?
- What would be the consequences if...?
- How would you feel about...?

These are particularly useful in the 'new understanding' phase of the mentoring process to help reframe problems which the mentee may be getting stuck on. Use with caution, however, as these can disguise advice or turn into leading questions (see below).

Link questions

Questions which connect ideas or events, or seek to understand the connection between them.

- So, if you say you cannot do...what will that mean for...?
- How will you...if...?
- You say you do this, and that this often happens...Are these two things connected?

These are also useful for prompting new understanding and helping the mentee explore cause and effect.

But beware of the following:

Closed questions

Questions that generally have a yes or no answer. Excessive use of these can turn a conversation into a session of 20 questions, particularly with a partner who is shy or inclined to be monosyllabic. Used in moderation, however, for clarification or probing, they can help to avoid misunderstandings.

- So this happened last week?
- Are you saying you have tried this?
- Will you have this done by...?

Leading questions

Questions which invite a particular answer by the way they are phrased.

- So, you think your problem is...?
- I expect you were just feeling a bit off, were you?
- I guess at that point you...did you?

These are to be watched for and avoided at all times, as they can disguise real issues and patronise the mentee.

TASK

Let's take a look at an abbreviated mentoring discussion and see if you can spot the different types of question and whether they are being used in the right places.

Toby Ken Wanobi	*So Sky, what would you like to talk about today?*
Sky Lukewarmer	*Well, lately I've been finding it difficult to use the Force.*
Toby Ken Wanobi	*Umm, I see. Why don't you tell me about it?*
Sky Lukewarmer	*Well, in the heat of battle, everything seems to be moving so fast that I keep missing my target altogether.*
Toby Ken Wanobi	*What seems different from previous sorties?*
Sky Lukewarmer	*I suppose I just lose concentration for a moment.*
Toby Ken Wanobi	*Are you getting enough sleep?*
Sky Lukewarmer	*Yes.*
Toby Ken Wanobi	*Oh... well... what do you mean by losing concentration?*
Sky Lukewarmer	*I keep thinking about why my father doesn't look anything like me.*
Toby Ken Wanobi	*Anything else?*
Sky Lukewarmer	*Yes, I get these strange thoughts every time I hear Garth Wader wheezing.*
Toby Ken Wanobi	*So you think Garth Wader has something to do with your father?*

Sky Lukewarmer	*No, not remotely.*
Toby Ken Wanobi	*Whoops... okay, so are you saying you find your mind wandering about unconnected concerns when you feel you should be focusing on flying your jetfighter?*
Sky Lukewarmer	*Yes, that's right.*
Toby Ken Wanobi	*What do you suppose would happen if you could anticipate these distracting thoughts and block them?*
Sky Lukewarmer	*Well I guess I'd find it easier to maintain the Force... and I'd remember where I left my light sabre.*
Toby Ken Wanobi	*And what might you do to try to improve your concentration?*
Sky Lukewarmer	*I suppose I could spend more time rehearsing flight tactics, and visualising successful bombing runs. I could also remove those pictures of Princess Camilla from the cockpit...*
Toby Ken Wanobi	*So can you commit to trying out these changes before we meet again in two weeks' time?*
Sky Lukewarmer	*Yes, absolutely. May the Force be with me!*
Toby Ken Wanobi	*Yeah, whatever...*

A word about 'why?'...

Finally, a word about 'why'. You may be familiar with the following lines from Rudyard Kipling:

I have six faithful serving men,

Who taught me all I know.

Their names are: What and Where and When,

And How and Why and Who?

Often quoted in interview training, this is largely sound advice to stick to open questions. However, it is generally acknowledged that 'why' questions should be used with caution. This is because, of all the questioning words, it can be the most challenging and potentially aggressive, particularly when applied to a person's motives. Compare the following sets of questions:

- Why do you say that?
- Why did you take that approach?
- Why are you so upset about...?

and

- Why do you think that might have happened?
- Why might she be reacting in that way?
- Why do birds suddenly appear...?

The second group of questions are helpful and non-threatening attempts to explore particular events. But the first group question an individual's motives and, phrased in that way, may meet with a defensive response. If a strong challenge is what you are after, and is appropriate, then fine, but otherwise an alternative might be to opt for a different W, like this:

- What makes you...?
- Where do you think... comes from?

Reflecting back

Building on the role of sounding board, which we mentioned earlier, you may find that sometimes the most useful and powerful thing a mentor can do is act as a mirror that allows the mentee to see and hear themselves as others see and hear them.

In its simplest form this consists of simply repeating the mentee's own statements in the form of a question, a technique which could quickly become annoying in the extreme.

Mentee *The presence of an observer in the classroom always makes me so nervous.*

Mentor *You feel nervous in the presence of an observer?*

Mentee *Yes, it's like I forget what a good teacher I really am.*

Mentor *So, you forget what a good teacher you are?*

Mentee *Is it me, or is there an echo in here?*

Of course you wouldn't do it like that. The trick here, apart from using the technique sparingly, is to try to 'add value' to the reflection. So, rather than simply *parroting* back what the mentee has said, we should demonstrate that we are *trying to understand* what is being said.

Mentee *The presence of an observer in the classroom always makes me so nervous.*

Mentor *So you feel more nervous when an observer is in the classroom, even though nothing else is different?*

Mentee *Yes, it's like I forget what a good teacher I really am.*

Mentor *You lose your usual confidence in your abilities?*

This is a tricky balance between helping to improve understanding and putting words into the mentee's mouth. But, done well, reflecting back can encourage the mentee to take an observer's eye view of their feelings and behaviour and see them in a new light.

Summarising

Although on the face of it a pretty basic interview skill, along with listening and questioning, summarising is a little trickier in mentoring due to the question of who does it and when.

It can be helpful at the start of a mentoring session to establish where things have got to and help to agree an agenda for the meeting. Equally, it can be useful during the 'exploration' phase to ensure mutual understanding of what is being discussed. It can help to capture learning during the 'new understanding' phase. And finally, of course, it can be used in action planning to summarise the whole discussion and agree a way forward.

So summarising does several things (I'm summarising here).

- It helps us to remember where we've got to.
- It adds structure to the discussion.
- It ensures both parties have the same understanding of what has been said.
- It distils learning from the conversation.
- It promotes a conclusion and gets commitment to action.

The key thing is that it does not have to remain the exclusive preserve of the mentor. Part of the skill of summarising is knowing when to get the mentee to do it. There are no hard and fast rules here, but a good mentor should always consider the following.

- Will getting the mentee to summarise where we have got to at the start of a meeting help to get them talking, test their understanding of and commitment to the process and enable me to check we're on the same track?
- Do I feel I can summarise what the mentee has been exploring here, or am I struggling and therefore better off getting her to do it?
- Am I positive that I've understood what the mentee has expressed, or should I verify my understanding?
- Has the mentee spotted the learning point here, in which case I can helpfully summarise it, or is it still sinking in, in which case she should?
- Am I confident of my mentee's commitment to this action plan, or should I get him to summarise it so I can be sure he's taken it on board?

TASK

Now we're going to eavesdrop on part of a mentoring session (below) which takes place in an FE college refectory between Talia and her mentor, Bob. Talia is a recently appointed team leader in ILT (information learning technology), and Bob is a team leader of long experience, also in the School of Technology. Read it through and consider your answers to the following questions.

1. To what extent does Bob utilise four of the skills we have just been discussing: listening, questioning, reflecting back and summarising?

2. Were there any missed opportunities where Bob could have usefully brought these skills into play and if so, where?

3. Is there anything you would have done differently from the way Bob did it?

You may find it useful to make notes of your answers to these questions, so that you can compare them with what we have to say in the discussion which follows.

Bob	Right. Go on, then.
Talia	Sorry?
Bob	Go on. I'm listening. I've only got 20 minutes.
Talia	Oh. Right. Well, I think last time we were talking about –
Bob	Never mind last time. What's on your mind this week? Come on.
Talia	This week? Well, this week's not been too bad, really. It's more the sort of long-term things that are worrying me. I've got this presentation to do to the senior management team and I'm really not very good at that sort of thing. So it's on my mind all the time, and I find I can't concentrate on other stuff because of it. I don't want to stand there in front of the SMT and forget what I was going to say and make an idiot of myself. I don't know why, but I'm just so bad at presentations.
Bob	Can't you get out of it?
Talia	Well, not really, no. It's part of the job, isn't it?
Bob	I shouldn't let it worry you. If you make a mess of it they'll perhaps not ask you again. Anything else?
Talia	Oh. Well, I'm trying to organise some professional development sessions in online tutoring, but I can't seem to drum up any enthusiasm from the team. Nobody wants to stay on late for them, but we haven't got any time on the timetable when we're all available, so it's going to have to be after work. And I was wondering –
Bob	No point. I tried offering some sessions a couple of years ago. No interest. Waste of time.
Talia	Yes, but things have moved on so fast in the last couple of years. Online learning is like a norm now in some areas and if we don't update our skills, people are going to go elsewhere. We're going to lose students. What I need is some way to get the team enthused about it. Mind you, I suppose, now I think about it, I could do the online training online. Makes sense, doesn't it?
Bob	Sorry. What? I was miles away there. Say that bit again.

DISCUSSION

1. To what extent does Bob utilise the four complex skills we have just been discussing: listening, questioning, reflecting back, summarising?

   You will have noticed immediately that Bob isn't much of a listener, nor does he ask many open questions. He hasn't even grasped the primary skills for mentoring that we've just been looking at.

2. Were there any missed opportunities where Bob could have usefully brought these skills into play and if so, where?

   You will have noticed that there were numerous opportunities to bring these skills to bear. He could have allowed Talia to summarise where they had got to in the last session, as she was beginning to do. He could have used more open questioning to explore Talia's anxiety about the presentation. He could have summarised and reflected back to her what she was saying about her professional development plans for her team, both to demonstrate his understanding and to help her gain a clearer perspective. Most of all, he could have listened more and pontificated less. He could have done all this and more; but he didn't. Hopefully, someone will go out and buy him this book. We shall be having a look in Chapter Seven at how evaluation strategies can be implemented to identify and address cases of ineffective mentoring like this one.

3. Is there anything you would have done differently from the way Bob did it?

Having read this far, of course you would. Let's give Talia a new mentor now – Ivan, who we met in the last chapter – and re-run the mentoring session.

Task

Using the notes you've made, see how your approach would compare with Ivan's.

Ivan *So, Talia, before we talk about how things are going shall we just look at where we were up to last time?*

Talia *Erm, I think we were talking about the problem with rooms and how I was trying to – you know – sort out the timetabling so the big groups have enough machines and the small groups aren't taking up rooms with lots of machines in them.*

Ivan *So how's that going?*

Talia *Sorted! Well, sort of sorted.*

Ivan *Excellent. Good for you. I'm really pleased that's coming together. How are things otherwise?*

Talia *To be honest it's the sort of long-term things that are worrying me now. I've got this presentation to do to the senior management team and I'm really not very good at that sort of thing. So it's on my mind all the time, and I find I can't concentrate on other stuff because of it. I don't want to stand there in front of the SMT and forget what I was going to say and make an idiot of myself. I don't know why, but I'm just so bad at presentations.*

Ivan *So, you're saying you get nervous at presentations and this affects your performance?*

Talia *Well, I can imagine standing there, getting all nervous and sweaty, and knowing I need to make an impression but making completely the wrong one...*

Ivan *You know, I've seen you teach. I've seen you stand up in front of groups of really difficult students – even more difficult than the SMT – no, don't laugh – and we've both agreed you're pretty impressive. So what is preventing you from doing the same to a group of senior managers?*

Talia *It's just I've never done it before.*

Ivan *Well, how would you feel if you had been able to try your presentation out with someone first? Have a sort of trial run? Get a bit of feedback?*

Talia *That would be so cool.*

Ivan   Okay. Let's sort out dates for us to do that together before we finish.

Talia   Yes please. And listen, I'm trying to organise some professional development sessions in online tutoring, but I can't seem to drum up any enthusiasm from the team. Nobody wants to stay on late for them, but we haven't got any time on the timetable when we're all available, so it's going to have to be after work. And I was wondering whether you had any advice or bright ideas?

Ivan   Online tutoring skills? Just what we need. Good timing. But yeah, you can understand people wanting to get home, not wanting to hang around for professional development sessions when they're tired. What alternatives are there to conventional taught sessions? Can we try a bit of lateral thinking?

Talia   I suppose, now I think about it, I could do the online training online. Makes sense, doesn't it?

Ivan   Great idea! And I tell you what: I bet it'd go down well with the SMT, something innovative like that. Are there any benefits in including it in your presentation? Why don't you just run through where we've got to so far on this?

DISCUSSION

I think we'd all like Ivan for a mentor, wouldn't we? And hopefully this is – more or less – the way you too would have done it. Did you pick out Ivan's use of essential skills? Here are some examples.

Listening

Lots of evidence that Ivan is actively listening:

Excellent. Good for you. I'm really pleased that's coming together.

Online tutoring skills? Just what we need. Good timing.

Questioning

Ivan uses a good combination of questions: open, probing and hypothetical:

So how's that going? How are things otherwise?

So what is preventing you from doing the same to a group of senior managers?

Well, how would you feel if you had been able to try your presentation out with someone first?

Reflecting back

Ivan reflects back to Talia her statement about being bad at presentations:

So, you're saying you get nervous at presentations and this affects your performance?

Summarising

Ivan encourages Talia to summarise their previous discussion as a starting point for this one, and then asks her to summarise towards the end:

> *Before we talk about how things are going shall we just look at where we were up to last time?*

> *Why don't you just run through where we've got to so far on this?*

Did you notice also the way in which Ivan avoids being cast in the role of 'rescuer'? Look at this exchange again, edited down to the essentials:

Talia *I was wondering whether you had any advice or bright ideas?*

Ivan *What alternatives are there to conventional taught sessions? Can we try a bit of lateral thinking?*

It would appear from this that Ivan probably already has in mind the idea about providing the professional development online; but, by use of judicious questioning, he is careful to allow Talia to arrive at this answer. He clearly recognises that she needs to come up with her own solutions rather than build up a dependency on her mentor to have all the right answers.

One of the other issues which this scenario reinforces is that a successful mentoring relationship is not necessarily dependent on mentor and mentee sharing a subject area. Bob and Talia shared an expertise in ILT, but this proved to be no advantage compared with Ivan's sound grasp of mentoring skills.

CLOSE FOCUS

You may find it useful, for revision purposes, to look through both scenarios again, this time evaluating Bob and Ivan against the approach to mentoring we covered in Chapter Two. Do they appear to have the right sort of attitude to mentoring? How does the process compare with the model we discussed?

Is Talia a 'good mentee'?

Summary

So now we have taken a look at some of the essential skills of mentoring. In this chapter we have discussed the importance of rapport in building trust and providing personal reflective space within which the mentee can take time honestly to appraise their own experiences.

We have also focused on four other skills: listening, questioning, reflecting back and summarising.

There are a number of ways we can demonstrate active listening, including regular eye contact, encouraging noises, body language, summarising and focusing entirely on the mentee.

We can use a combination of open questions, probing questions, link questions and hypothetical questions to encourage our mentee to explore issues thoroughly and extract new learning. Closed questions have their place, used sparingly, but we should beware of leading questions.

As well as demonstrating active listening, the skills of reflecting back and summarising can help the mentee to take an observer's eye view of their feelings and behaviour, as well as ensuring a common understanding, distilling learning from events and getting commitment to action. Remember, it need not be the mentor who summarises.

References and further reading

Egan, G (2002) *The Skilled Helper*. Pacific Grove, CA USA: Brooks/Cole, Thomson Learning.

Rogers, C (1983) *Freedom to Learn for the 80s*. Columbus, OH: Merrill.

This chapter is designed to help you to:

- identify and apply some of the more complex skills that will prove useful in a mentoring situation;

- consider ways in which this more advanced range of skills can be used to improve the effectiveness of mentoring in a Further Education college or similar organisation in the Lifelong Learning sector;

- reflect on some of the ethical issues which mentors must be aware of in relation to their role;

- consider what happens when a mentoring relationship comes to an end.

Further skills for mentoring

In Chapter Three we explored some of the skills essential to mentors, such as building rapport, listening, questioning, summarising and reflecting. In this chapter we are going to look at some further skills which can be used to enhance the effectiveness of mentoring. These include:

- challenging;
- reframing;
- walking the tightrope.

First let's explain exactly what we mean by each of these, and then we'll go on to explore them in more detail, using examples and illustrations along the way, to identify how these skills can be used to enhance the mentoring process.

- Challenging is the skilful use of questions or statements to make the mentee reflect more carefully on what they are saying. They may be making assumptions about themselves or others, or perhaps failing to recognise aspects of their own behaviour which are preventing them from achieving their aims. Challenging can be threatening and needs to be used carefully.

- Reframing is a way of encouraging mentees to look at events and behaviour from a different perspective, to put themselves in another's shoes, or see the positive and negative consequences of various options. It often goes hand-in-hand with challenging and we look at the two together here.

- Walking the tightrope is our way of expressing the many conflicting impulses that a mentor may experience when trying to help someone develop. We believe that a greater awareness of these potential conflicts is a first step towards managing them successfully.

Challenging and reframing

To understand the purpose of challenging and reframing we need to go back to the question of self-knowledge, which we raised in Chapter Two while looking at the *exploration* stage of the mentoring process. We all have blind spots – things others may recognise about us, but that we don't see ourselves. A useful way to think about this is by having a careful look at the diagram below, usually referred to as Johari's Window. You may be familiar with it already, particularly if you have been involved in training for counselling skills.

> ## TASK
>
> Look at the diagram and explanation below, and then see if you can categorise the following cases in terms of Johari's Window.

1. Dina's mentor, Ivan, has excellent time-management skills. He is well aware of this and so is everyone else.
2. Mark is proving to be a competent and even charismatic teacher. Everyone around him recognises this, but he isn't yet confident enough to see it in himself.
3. Dina is a skilled and empathetic listener and will make an excellent mentor herself. Dina hasn't recognised this in herself, and neither has anyone else – yet!
4. Mark's mentor feels threatened by Mark. She lacks confidence in herself as a teacher, but no one else realises this.

Johari's Window

	KNOWN BY YOU	NOT KNOWN BY YOU	
KNOWN BY OTHERS	The public you	Your blind spots	Positives and negatives
NOT KNOWN BY OTHERS	The mask	Your unknown potential	

What the Johari's Window diagram illustrates is that there are aspects of our personality, behaviour, attitude and so on that are obvious both to us and to those around us, just as there are things we may mask from others, covering our lack of confidence or discomfort. In the same way we all display behaviours and traits which we are unaware of, but which are very apparent to others, just as we have untapped talents and resources which remain hidden to everyone, even ourselves. Good mentoring should help us learn more about ourselves and expand our public face along both axes, thus revealing more of our hidden potential.

DISCUSSION

If we apply this to the four examples given above, we arrive at the following categorisation.

1. Dina's mentor, Ivan, has excellent time-management skills. He is well aware of this, and so is everyone else = *aspects of our personality, behaviour, attitude and so on that are obvious both to us and to those around us.*

2. Mark is proving to be a competent and even charismatic teacher. Everyone around him recognises this, but he isn't yet confident enough to see it in himself = *behaviours and traits which we are unaware of, but which are very apparent to others.*

3. Dina is a skilled and empathetic listener and will make an excellent mentor herself. Dina hasn't recognised this in herself, and neither has anyone else – yet! = *we have untapped talents and resources which remain hidden to everyone, even ourselves.*

4. Mark's mentor feels threatened by Mark's evident skills as a teacher. She lacks confidence in herself as a teacher, but no one else realises this = *there are things we may mask from others; covering our lack of confidence or discomfort.*

There are several ways in which a mentor may choose to help their mentee address their blind spots. They may give the mentee some feedback, a process we examine in more detail in the next chapter. Alternatively, they may *challenge* something the mentee appears to be taking for granted. In other words, they may use the questioning skills we looked at earlier specifically to make the mentee think more critically about what they have been saying.

Take a look at the following brief extract from a mentoring session between Gordon and his mentor, Zulfi. Gordon is an experienced teacher who has been assigned a mentor as part of a pilot scheme for continuing professional development. What is Gordon's blind spot, and how does Zulfi deal with this?

Zulfi	*Well, Gordon, you've mentioned several times now your ambitions to be a head of department at some point. What new or different skills do you think this might entail?*
Gordon	*Oh, I think I've been teaching long enough now to pretty much know what this department needs in order to function properly. I've been here longer than just about any of the other staff. People look up to me, you know? They see me as a sort of father figure. I already spend a lot of my time sorting out the newer, younger folks when they get themselves in a mess over timetabling or marking, or whatever. They can always trust old Gordon to get 'em out of the mire.*
Zulfi	*You seem to be saying that a good head of department mainly needs to be more experienced at teaching than everyone else. Is that how you see it?*

Gordon	Well let's face it, it helps, doesn't it? I've seen these wet-behind-the-ears types they parachute into some of these roles, and they've far less classroom experience than I've got.
Zulfi	But then how much time do they spend in the classroom?
Gordon	A lot less than the rest of us, obviously. I mean they've got management responsibilities, haven't they, inter-departmental committees, stuff outside the college.
Zulfi	What sort of skills and abilities do you think all that is drawing on then?
Gordon	Goodness knows...schmoozing and talking b****s, as far as I can tell.
Zulfi	Mmm...Why don't you tell me about some of the things you've had to organise outside of the classroom?
Gordon	What sort of things?
Zulfi	Well, you know, trips, conferences, external workshops. Maybe you've sat on some inter-departmental working parties or led some of the industrial liaison projects?
Gordon	No way. I can't be doing with all that. They pay me to teach, and that's what I do.
Zulfi	So do you think your colleagues see you more as an experienced teacher or as a potential leader?
Gordon	Well, I think they see me as both, but...yes, well you might have a point there, I suppose.

You will have noticed that Zulfi did not have to be argumentative or impolite, but equally he could not let Gordon continue to make false assumptions about his automatic eligibility for further promotion. This could possibly have prevented Gordon from undertaking the kind of personal development that he needed to move on in his career. (Of course, he may equally have come to the conclusion that his skills and lifestyle requirements best suited staying where he was.) By challenging Gordon's assumptions, in the interests of helping him think constructively about his own development, Zulfi may have avoided Gordon's career stagnating in misunderstandings and recrimination, or helped him formulate a career plan that was a better match for his skills and needs.

As important as helping our mentees to recognise and explore their blind spots is to remember that we, as mentors, almost certainly have blind spots of our own. Occasionally this lack of self-knowledge can get in the way of a productive and positive relationship between mentor and mentee. It can sometimes help the mentee to open up and address things they may be masking if the mentor shows they are willing to do the same. There is little worse than a mentor who only wants to talk about herself, but self-disclosure used sparingly can help build the trust to address sensitive issues. This is another reason why reflection on our mentoring practice is so important – how we do things and why – as we shall see in Chapter Six.

Challenging, then, is a critical skill in mentoring. Sometimes the greatest insights arise as a result of helping the mentee reframe the way they are thinking about something. But just as people may have a blind spot about what they *can* do, we all of us have blind spots about what we *cannot* do. These are often referred to as self-limiting beliefs. Some typical *self-limiting beliefs* are as follows.

- *Everyone has to like me* – I must always be loved and approved of by the most important people in my life.
- *I must be good at everything* – I must be competent in all situations, and talented in some important area of my life.
- *I have to get my own way* – things must go my way and my plans must always succeed.
- *I have to stay out of trouble* – if a situation is at all threatening I must be worried and wound-up about it. Things should not go wrong, and if they do, there should be quick and easy solutions.
- *Infamy, infamy. They've all got it in for me* – my misery is always the result of other people and outside forces.
- *I can be a spectator* – it is quite possible to be happy by being uncommitted, by avoiding and just being passive.
- *I am a product of my history* – how I act and feel today is entirely determined by what I did in the past.

(This list, originally by Albert Ellis (1998 and 1999) is adapted from Egan, 2002. If you would like to read more about self-limiting beliefs, you will find the full reference at the end of the chapter.)

Challenging any preconception or assumption can lead to greater insight, but questioning those beliefs about ourselves which limit our capacity to improve can be particularly powerful.

The mentor's skill is in spotting when the mentee is indulging in disempowering self-talk – talking themselves down – and 'victim' behaviour, transferring the responsibility for change onto anyone but themselves, and maybe casting the mentor in the role of rescuer; in other words, relying on the mentor to improve or change them. In the context of teacher and learner, this is a scenario that most of us will recognise: the learner who lacks confidence to engage with their learning and prefers to see it as entirely the teacher's responsibility.

There is a health warning, however. Challenging, and particularly challenging self-limiting beliefs, must be done in a spirit of compassion and humility. Almost all of us feel uncomfortable when we first read that list of self-limiting beliefs and it helps if we can remember that. Challenge should be specific, tactful and ideally focused on *underused strengths* rather than weaknesses. But it must also come from within the context of a trusting and empathetic relationship, and an attitude on the part of the challenger – the mentor – that they are on the side of the mentee and confident of the mentee's capacity to change. This is the essence of the critical friend role played by the mentor. Clutterbuck and Megginson (1999) have the following advice.

Challenge the behaviour, not the person.

Challenge their assumptions, not their intellect.

Challenge their perceptions, not their judgement.

Challenge their values, not their value.

(You'll find the full reference, if you'd like to read more, at the end of this chapter.)

Walking the tightrope

We've explored some basic skills and some more complex skills associated with mentoring, but good mentoring is more than simply the sum of these techniques. The real skill lies not simply in mastering a set of strategies. Successful mentoring involves a *balancing act*, the reconciliation of seemingly opposite impulses, either of which, on their own, can be as damaging as they are helpful. For example, when we looked at questioning skills in Chapter Three we acknowledged how our desire to help someone can result in us suggesting a solution, rather than helping them develop their own. This is a difficult thing to teach. One's instinct for it grows from practice, and also from reflection – an issue we shall be looking at in more detail in Chapter Six. Meanwhile we have given this section the heading *walking the tightrope* in order to emphasise the *balancing act* required to mentor effectively. We're now going to look at some of the areas where we need to get the balance right, provide steady support and guidance and – hopefully – avoid any nasty falls for our mentee or ourselves.

> ### Task
>
> Read carefully through the six guidelines for balanced mentoring given below and then have a look at the description of a mentoring situation which follows.
>
> 1. What examples, if any, can you identify in this account of the six guidelines being followed?
>
> 2. Can you find instances of other mentoring skills being put into practice here? If so, what are they?

Guidelines for balanced mentoring

1. Balancing preparation and going with the flow

Preparation for a meeting with the mentee is one of the points at which balance is crucial. Too little preparation and the mentor may miss opportunities to use their own knowledge resources to help the mentee.

Thinking about potentially useful models, information sources or network contacts beforehand may help. However, we have to watch our motives here. Planning and preparation based on assumptions about the mentee's needs may serve more to allay your own anxiety and result in you imposing your agenda on the discussion, at the expense of the mentee's.

2. Balancing exploration of the issues and committing to action

Again, balance is important. Insufficient attention to the exploration stage (see Chapter Two) may cause the mentor to misjudge the key factors in the mentee's development, to focus on the superficial rather than engaging with the underlying causes of whatever it is the mentee is trying to resolve. Conversely, extended exploration can become self-indulgent and comforting, because ultimately learning and change come from taking action, from leaving one's comfort zone and risking failure. Moving from exploration to action is a key dynamic in the mentoring process.

3. Balancing overview and context with specific experiences

The balance between exploration and action is closely linked to this question of moving between the general and the particular. Deliberately spending time helping a mentee to generate her own vision of success, articulate her own dream, can be key to motivating that individual and setting their transition in some kind of context. However, taking too broad a perspective can blind us to the detail. We miss important stories and critical incidents, vital to the mentee's learning. Sometimes as much can be gained from examination of one crucial piece of behaviour – that is, concentrating on something in depth – as it can from meditating on our overall learning goals. The successful mentor constantly reminds herself of the need to alternate between general principles and critical incidents and examples.

4. Balancing being helpful and not being too directive

Mentors are faced with the challenge of responding adequately to their mentee's expectation of help, whilst maintaining the individual's sense of ownership, responsibility and agency. Information and insights from the mentor's own experience can be useful, provided:

- they are customised (i.e. relevant), and add value;
- they are genuinely aimed at helping the coachee/mentee;
- they require some action by the recipient (e.g. article to read, activity to try, framework to apply, etc.).

Given that a mentoring relationship may call upon the mentor occasionally to fulfil a coaching role, there will be times when it is appropriate to raise different ideas or options. Generally this is best done in the form of a question ('have you ever thought of...?', 'what might happen if...?'). An even gentler alternative is to get the mentee to picture potential role models and think about what they might do.

5. Balancing challenge and the 'warm bath'

Without sufficient challenge a mentoring relationship can easily become just a comfortable form of therapy, a 'warm bath' in which the learner off-loads their responsibility for action along with their anxieties and problems. The reason it is problematic, however, is that the degree of challenge which is appropriate and helpful varies from mentee to mentee. So, once again, do not be afraid of stepping back from the process and asking how challenging they want you to be. Of course, bear in mind that this will not always result in an honest answer. The 'give it to me straight, Doc' merchant may still get a bit shirty if you actually do. Likewise, the mentee who rather likes a warm bath will probably tell you you're really being quite challenging enough, thank you.

6. Balancing feelings and rationality

Learning, like all change, is an emotional as well as rational experience. Mentors must not lose sight of the need to explore both dimensions when helping learners to change and develop. The mentor's role is at least partly to encourage confidence and positive thinking. We miss out on a significant part of decision-making if we ignore emotions, and often the best insights come from understanding how one *feels* about an issue, as well as what one thinks of it.

Sam's story

How have I enjoyed being a mentor? Well, it's been mixed, really. Clifford hasn't been the easiest of people to work with. He's always got some tale of woe, you know. Take the other day…

Sam   *Now then, Cliff. How are we doing? Are we going to have a word about your action plan today? That's what we decided we'd do I think, isn't it?*

Cliff   *I think we did, yeah. But I don't think I've brought it with me. I've had such a hell of a week. That so-called section leader, he's at me the whole time. 'Where's this?' 'Have you done that?' 'Why isn't this finished?' Blah, blah, blah. And I go, 'Look, mate, there's only so many hours in a day.'*

Sam   *Don't worry. I've got a copy of your action plan here. Now, let's have a look where we're up to.*

Cliff   *I don't know when I'm supposed to be thinking about action plans and that. When am I supposed to have time for all that?*

Sam   *Well, we've got a bit of time for it now, so shall we just –*

Cliff   *You might have a bit of time. You want to see the pile of marking waiting for me. I would say 'on my desk', but I haven't got a desk, have I? I have to share a desk, don't I?*

Sam   *Yes, I remember you telling me. That must be difficult.*

Cliff   *Difficult? It's bloody impossible. How am I supposed to do the job when they don't even give me my own desk?*

Sam   *That's one of the problems, isn't it, when you're part-time. I remember it well.*

Cliff   *Were you part-time then?*

> **Sam** *When I started, yes. When the kids were small. It's a hard life, Clifford, but –*
>
> **Cliff** *How many kids have you got, then?*
>
> **Sam** *Five. Right, come on. Let's have a look at how we're doing with this action plan.*
>
> **Cliff** *Five? Bloody hell! One's bad enough. Still not getting a night's sleep.*
>
> **Sam** *Really? So, this action plan –*
>
> **Cliff** *Haven't had a night's sleep in two years.*
>
> **Sam** *I can sympathise with that, Cliff. But look, we've got 30 minutes set aside for this meeting, and I think the most helpful thing would be if we focus on the action plan, because that's something we've got to do if you're going to get your Stage 2; and then maybe next time we could have a chat about time management, because clearly you're having a lot of demands made on your time and I really sympathise with that. So action plan, yeah?*
>
> **Cliff** *Yeah. Well, I think I'd probably like to change my action plan.*
>
> **Sam** *Ah. Why?*
>
> **Cliff** *I think I need to think it through a bit more; talk it through a bit more with you, before I commit myself, you know? I need to think about the whole thing – where I'm going with it; is it really for me, you know?*
>
> **Sam** *I thought we had talked it through, Cliff. We've spent our last three sessions looking at the wider view. Now you've decided to commit, we need to be exploring areas for development, strengths to build on – all of that. I think the time has come to take the plunge. If you don't take the plunge now, you're going to hold up everything else: your teaching practice documentation, your assignment two, your reflective journal…*
>
> **Cliff** *Okay, okay. Point taken.*
>
> **Sam** *Yeah? Because it's not that I don't sympathise with the difficulties. I know you're having a hard time. And I agree we need to talk some more about that. Time management and all the rest. But there's a deadline for this action plan, and I don't want to see you fail the qualification just because we didn't get this done.*
>
> **Cliff** *I know.*
>
> **Sam** *So. Let's get this filled in. First, what would you say your strengths are, Cliff?*
>
> **Cliff** *Well, for starters I think it's fair to say I'm a really clear thinker. My concentration is like a laser beam. When something needs doing, I do it. Job done. No messing about. That's me.*

Discussion

1. Balance between preparation and going with the flow

Sam had clearly planned for the session to focus on Clifford's action plan. She goes with the flow for a short time, allowing Clifford to express the things that are currently on his mind; but she keeps returning tenaciously to the plan. Was she right to do this, do you think? Is this what you would have done? What reasons would you give? Might she risk missing other, less apparent issues that Cliff needs to resolve?

2. *Balance between exploration and action*

It becomes clear that Clifford and Sam have spent a considerable time previously in the exploration stage. Here Sam insists firmly that they turn their attention to action. Do you think she is right?

3. *Balance between breadth and depth*

We learn that this mentee has spent a lot of time discussing the wider issues with his mentor: *I need to think about the whole thing – where I'm going with it; is it really for me.* Sam feels it's time to focus in depth on specific issues to do with Clifford's professional development. Do you think she is getting the balance right here?

4. *Balance between directive and non-directive*

Sam is quite directive in this encounter. Occasionally she allows Clifford to take the conversation off track: *How many kids have you got, then?* But she soon steers them back on track: *I can sympathise with that, Cliff. But look, we've got 30 minutes set aside for this meeting, and I think the most helpful thing would be if we focus on the action plan.* Do you think this degree of directiveness is justified? What would you have done?

5. *Balance between challenge and warm bath*

Sam appears to sympathise and empathise: *That's one of the problems, isn't it, when you're part-time. I remember it well.* But she's clearly not prepared simply to listen to Clifford's tale of woe and dole out sympathy and lend an uncritical ear. She has plans for this mentoring session and she's fairly vigorous about the way she imposes them. *Maybe next time we could have a chat about time management, because clearly you're having a lot of demands made on your time and I really sympathise with that. So action plan, yeah?* In your view does this hit the right note?

6. *Balance between emotion and rationality*

We've seen that Sam can empathise with Clifford on some issues, but she is clearly putting a limit on the amount of time she's going to spend in listening to how Clifford feels. Part of her remit is to support her mentee in gaining his teaching qualification, and we see her taking a rational approach as she focuses on this prime directive. Do you think she got the balance right here?

CLOSE FOCUS

If you are currently a mentor, perhaps you might use these balance scales as a start point for jointly reviewing one of your current mentoring relationships with your mentee. Are you striking the right balance, or are there things your mentee would like to do more of or less of?

To summarise, some tips on walking this tightrope would be:

- Ensure the purpose of any preparation is to tune in to the learner and help them prepare themselves, not to ease your own anxiety by pre-empting the agenda.

- Do not be reticent about challenging, provided that you have established a rapport and a positive, supportive environment through reinforcement and focusing on the individual's strengths to overcome obstacles.

- Recognise when the mentee needs to move to action in order to learn. Do not expect every encounter to be deep and meaningful. Be happy with being pragmatic and action-orientated, if that helps most.

- Address both 'being' and 'doing', helping the learner focus on feelings as well as rational thought, and moving readily between general principles and specific examples.

- Avoid over-direction leading to dependency by evaluating sessions with the question 'Is the learner better able to learn and help themselves than before?'

CLOSE FOCUS

Having read the summary above, what would your final evaluation be of Sam's performance as a mentor?

Ethics

We have seen how mentoring can be enormously helpful but, as you may have concluded from some of our examples, it also has the potential to do harm. In this respect it is no different from other types of one-to-one helping relationship.

It is important, therefore, that we take a little time to touch on the subject of ethics. We cannot hope to do justice to such a complex topic in the space we have available here, but if you want to study this further there are some helpful references at the end of this chapter. A good start point would be the European Mentoring and Coaching Council's Code of Ethics. You'll find the website reference at the end of this chapter, too.

So what are some of the pitfalls we need to be aware of if we are to be responsible and professional mentors? Let us look at the four Cs:

- control;
- competence;
- conflict of interest;
- confidentiality.

Control

Mentors are often in the position to exert considerable influence over their mentees. They may be more experienced, more senior, and at the very least will have been around the college long enough to know far more of the personalities, systems and politics. It is not difficult, even with the best of intentions, to impose our own agenda, opinions, standards and solutions on a mentee. The temptation to play God, to somehow change the mentee, even for what we may see as the better, is a dangerous impulse. Mentors need to ask themselves whether they are allowing their own sense of self-importance to take precedence over a genuine concern for helping the mentee find their own way. Mentees may unwittingly contribute to the problem by saying only what they think their mentor wants to hear. In its more extreme forms, control may turn into harassment, or other forms of discrimination. Conversely, mentors may find themselves mentoring colleagues who are more experienced and/or more senior than themselves. This is another situation in which issues to do with power and control may inhibit a successful relationship.

Competence

We saw in Chapter One how one mark of a good mentor is their commitment to continuous learning. It goes without saying, therefore, that a mentor will always look to improve their skills in mentoring. One way of doing this is to have a supervisor. This is a sort of mentor to the mentor, who can help them develop their skills and talk through tricky or troubling mentoring issues. We talk about this more in Chapter Eight with regard to setting up mentoring schemes.

As well as developing our competence in mentoring, however, we must as mentors beware of straying into areas which are not our expertise. The role is a broad one, as we have seen, and we may find mentees confiding in us about subjects which we are unqualified to deal with. In responding to this sort of self-disclosure, we must recognise the boundaries of our own skills and knowledge and avoid playing the amateur psychologist or marriage counsellor.

Conflict of interest

There may be times when a mentor feels unable to address a particular issue objectively with their mentee because of their own stake in the matter. For example, the colleague they are having such trouble with is a personal friend of yours, or they confess to professionally reprehensible behaviour which you feel should be reported. Perhaps the most common source of this difficulty is the relationship between the mentor, the mentee and the mentee's immediate manager. If these are three different people, the mentor may find themselves called upon to help the mentee resolve relationship difficulties with their boss. If the mentor is their boss, then such matters may never get addressed. If you are assessing a probationary teacher, according to an agenda devised by the college, does this inhibit your ability to mentor them in a non-judgemental way?

Confidentiality

A subject we mentioned in the context of contracting with the mentee, confidentiality is an important element of the trust that is required for a successful mentoring relationship. We must be clear about the limits of that confidentiality, particularly where assessments and records are concerned, and agree circumstances when confidentiality cannot be guaranteed. What do you think some of these circumstances might be? Finally, mentors must respect the confidentiality of the mentoring relationship beyond the point at which it ends.

DISCUSSION

Think about your own mentoring role and discuss these questions, perhaps with your fellow mentors.

- Is a mentor's principal duty to the success and reputation of the college or to the development of the individual mentee?
- Do we measure the success of mentoring by our own standards and those of the college, or by the mentee's happiness?
- Is any form of help acceptable in mentoring, provided the mentee welcomes it?

Endings

So far we have focused on what happens when mentoring begins and what it might look like in full flow. But we have not yet talked about what happens when it comes to an end.

Remember Bob and Talia, whom we met in Chapter Three? Time has moved on and they are coming to the end of their last planned mentoring session (amazingly Talia has stuck with it, probably out of pity).

Bob   *So, Talia, let me just summarise what you're going to do...*

Talia   *Tell you what Bob, why don't I summarise it?*

Bob   *Well, okay, as it's our last session.*

Talia   *I'm going to read up on that stuff on open space events that you told me about, and I'm going to continue with my learning log, maybe reviewing it with my head of department every three or four months. Oh, and I'm definitely going to volunteer for that curriculum working party thing.*

Bob   *Great! Well, I expect you'll be wanting to get off.*

Talia   *Actually Bob, before I go, I just wanted to say... you know...*

Bob   *Oh, come along now, for goodness sake let's not get all sentimental. It's just a job, you know. I'll be mentoring someone else next week.*

Talia   *Yes, I know that, but all the same...*

> Bob *Look, I think you've really come on over the last year or so, honestly. I mean you were really all over the place when we first met, but now you're not. Well done!*
>
> Talia *Well thanks for... you know... everything...*
>
> Bob *Yes, fine, fine. Don't miss your next class now!...*

How do you think Bob and Talia are feeling at the end of that final exchange? Talia clearly wanted to thank Bob properly, despite his faults, but felt a little awkward about it. Far from making it any easier, Bob could not wait to get her out of the room, before any messy emotional stuff got in the way. It is likely that Talia is left feeling unsatisfied and a little guilty, and even Bob is probably masking his real feelings behind a veneer of no-nonsense detachment. Imagine you missed saying goodbye to your partner, child or other loved one before a long trip away. This sense of unfinished business is pretty much how Bob and Talia may be left feeling. So how do we prevent this?

There is no real formula for success here, other than to accept that we all need to go through some sort of closing ritual when any relationship comes to an end. We need to mark what has happened in some way. Not all formal mentoring relationships end abruptly, for example. Many simply change into a much more informal connection. Ex-mentors become members of our personal/professional network. They even become friends in some cases. In any event, this point in the relationship signifies that the mentee is becoming more self-sufficient so in a way it can be a beginning as well as an ending.

As with so many aspects of mentoring, self-awareness is helpful here. A lot of the potential awkwardness that Bob and Talia felt could have been defused if they had jointly acknowledged that something was coming to an end and they should mark it properly. How you do this is up to you. It might be a review and evaluation of the relationship, or a summary of the mentee's development. Bob's half-hearted attempt at positive reinforcement just made it look as though Talia was fishing for compliments. So perhaps you should agree the session up front and conduct a proper review. Some people mark these occasions with a drink, an exchange of cards or even token gifts. What matters is that the occasion is properly marked, the ritual is observed in some way.

Summary

In this chapter we have delved into some of the less obvious skills of mentoring. We have used the Johari Window model to show how mentors can challenge their mentees, in order to help them address blind spots or self-limiting beliefs. This is an approach which must be used skilfully and with caution, but above all it must be applied within the context of a caring and supportive relationship. Helping mentees to reframe events and behaviour, to see things in a new and different light can help them discover new skills, question long-standing preconceptions and maybe see the positive opportunity in a seemingly negative situation.

We have presented mentoring as something of a balancing act, to reconcile what can seem contradictory aims:

- preparation and going with the flow;
- exploration of the issues and committing to action;
- overview of context and specific experiences;
- being helpful and not being too directive;
- challenge and the 'warm bath';
- feelings and rationality.

We have examined some of the ethical dilemmas that might arise from helping relationship of this sort, focusing on the 4 Cs of control, competen conflict of interest and confidentiality.

Finally we have tried to illustrate how we all need to observe some sort of ritual when a mentoring relationship changes or comes to an end, and we have made some suggestions as to how mentors may choose to ease the transition for both parties.

References

Clutterbuck, D and Megginson, D (1999) *Mentoring Executives and Directors*. Oxford: Butterworth Heinemann (p152).

Egan, G (2002) *The Skilled Helper*. Pacific Grove, CA USA: Brooks/Cole, Thomson Learning.

Ellis, A (1999) *How to Make Yourself Happy and Remarkably Less Disturbable*. San Luis Obispo, CA: Impact.

For information on ethics in mentoring:

European Mentoring and Coaching Council website: **www.emccouncil.org.uk**

Johari Window information:

www.noogenesis.com/game_theory/johari/johari_window.html.

5. Coaching and feedback

CHAPTER OBJECTIVES

This chapter is designed to help you to:

- consider the role of coaching within a mentoring relationship;

- identify key issues in the giving and receiving of feedback;

- explore the implications of the fact that a significant part of the mentoring process in an FE setting consists of observation and feedback by the mentor in order to help with the development of practical classroom skills and good professional practice.

Clearly, giving feedback is a fundamental teaching skill, familiar to most readers of this book who will undoubtedly have used it in a classroom environment. However, faced with a colleague on a one-to-one basis, few if any of us find feedback easy. It might, therefore, be worthwhile to remind ourselves of how to use this important technique in the specific setting of a mentoring relationship.

Coaching and mentoring

We saw in Chapter One how mentoring can be seen as encompassing a wide range of roles, including coaching. Many would still argue about the differences between the two, and even about whether such distinctions are helpful or not. Nevertheless, as we made clear from the various roles outlined in the introduction to this book, mentors in FE are routinely called upon to assess classroom practice and give feedback to their mentees in order to help them improve their skills. This particular aspect of the mentor's role conforms to many of the widely-held characteristics of coaching. (Further thoughts about mentoring and coaching may be found in the books listed at the end of this chapter.)

The mentor's coaching role

- It is relatively *short term* in nature. Practice is observed, feedback is given, potential improvements are agreed and then implemented, all within a relatively short space of time.

- It is, by and large, *skills-based*. That is not to say that problems in classroom teaching are entirely matters of technique. The motivation and mood of the teacher, relationships with students and a myriad of other factors will influence success. A good mentor will recognise these and help the mentee address them too. But primarily, the purpose of classroom observation is to help hone skills, so in this context the mentor and mentee are focusing on the job in hand.

- The mentor has more *control* over what is discussed, perhaps even complete control. Often the mentor will be referring to standards and competency statements in order to structure their feedback and, whilst this does not prevent the teacher raising issues of particular concern, the ensuing discussion will at best be only partly determined by the mentee. Whereas, as we have seen, in some mentoring sessions the agenda is entirely the mentee's and they should generally be encouraged to take responsibility for this.

- The discussion between mentor and mentee is centred around *feedback,* which is based largely on *external observation,* as well as on the mentee's own reflections about their thoughts, feelings and actions. Good feedback taps into the mentee's reflexivity, as we shall see, but ultimately the observer is required to make their observations. That is, after all, the purpose of the session.

TASK

Take a look at the following mentoring conversation between Mary, a PGCE student on teaching practice and her mentor, Jenny. Think about the various ways in which this seems to conform to or differs from what you might call coaching.

Jenny *Hi there, Mary. Come in and sit down. You look a bit flustered.*

Mary *Yeah, sorry. It's been a bit of a week. Thanks for agreeing to see me at such short notice though.*

Jenny *Don't mention it. Glad to be of help. What exactly was it you wanted to talk about?*

Mary *Oh I don't know. I'm just feeling a bit low at the moment. I'm not sure if this is the sort of teaching I want to do. I'm not even sure if I can be a teacher full-stop. I've had the most awful week. I'm supposed to move out of the flat next month and I can't find any temporary accommodation for love nor money. My Mum's poorly again and that Sean bloke seems to delight in baiting me in class and making me look a prat in front of everyone.*

Jenny *Gosh, there's a lot of stuff going on there, Mary. Where do you think we should start? How about this idea that you'll never be a teacher? I seem to remember your last assessment was very complimentary.*

Mary *I dunno. I just can't seem to concentrate on the job. It would be so much easier if I could just do something I'm already good at.*

Jenny *Some of us here think you're good at teaching. Do you remember the discussion we had about why you decided to do the PGCE?*

Mary *I know, I know. I wanted something that seemed fulfilling and worthwhile and it does still give me such a buzz to see people pick things up in class and develop their ideas and their knowledge. But I'm finding it so hard to motivate myself recently...*

Jenny *What has changed, Mary? I know Sean's always been a bit of a thorn in your side.*

Mary   *Well, I've got this media studies workshop I've said I'll run, and that's scaring me half to death, but then there's just too much going on, what with my Mum and everything.*

Jenny   *Perhaps we could break it down a bit, eh? What are the things you can actually do something about?*

Mary   *There's not much I can do about my Mum I suppose, but I would like to get to see her. Getting somewhere to live is the main thing at the moment and this damn workshop...*

Jenny   *If I could get Gurbinder, the guy who handles student accommodation problems, to spend some time with you, and we try to fix a time now to see your Mum, would that help take some of the immediate panic away?*

Mary   *Mmm yes, it would, I guess.*

Jenny   *We could then focus our minds on some of the job worries you've got.*

Mary   *Please. That would be really helpful.*

Jenny   *How do you feel about jacking in this teaching thing then?*

Mary   *Oh I don't know. I'm perhaps getting things out of proportion, but I wish I'd never volunteered for this workshop.*

Jenny   *Why don't we talk about how you might handle the workshop together, see if I can help you structure your thoughts. We could discuss some strategies for handling Sean as well, if you'd like. I can use some of the feedback from the last assessment to help perhaps.*

DISCUSSION

What did you spot? The agenda certainly began firmly in Mary's hands. She had arranged the meeting and she determined what they discussed. Some of the problems were perhaps a mix of long- and short-term issues, but the crisis of confidence over her future in teaching was certainly a long-term career decision. Likewise, the conversation covered much more than skills improvement. A number of things, some of them nothing to do with teaching, seemed to have conspired to distract Mary and undermine her confidence. Jenny concentrated on reminding Mary of the motivation behind her long-term ambitions, helping her to focus and put things in some sort of perspective, before offering active help.

Having said all this, however, Jenny did give Mary feedback, about her classroom assessment, to boost her confidence, and she did start to assert more control over the agenda towards the end of the extract where she began to move into what had all the makings of a potential coaching session. The point here is that these roles do not have sharply-defined edges. People who call themselves coaches will frequently engage in wider discussions about an individual's life, because their wellbeing inevitably affects their performance. Likewise, people who call themselves mentors will use coaching techniques to help develop skills and build confidence when this is appropriate.

Coaching process and skills

As we said earlier there are more models of the process in the coaching literature than in the mentoring literature. A number of these appear in the books listed at the end of this chapter. But if we summarise what it is that most of these helpful models have in common, we can see a lot of overlap with the mentoring process we described in Chapter One. Given the points made above, this is hardly surprising.

Contracting/rapport-building

Just as in other mentoring roles, both parties must have a common understanding of the boundaries of the relationship, who is responsible for what and how it will work. Issues such as confidentiality, expectations, meeting frequency and the duration of the relationship all need to be addressed in just the same way. Similarly, the parties need to get to know and trust one another.

Opportunity identification

Most coaching models involve some comparison between the coachee's aims and objectives and current reality, in order to determine where the opportunities for improvement and learning lie. This is an iterative process. You generally need to go around the loop more than once because current difficulties will spark possible objectives and vice-versa. It is often helpful here to explore the coachee's strengths, find out what they have tried successfully, not just where they have struggled.

Experimentation and development

Just as we talked about generating options in other mentoring roles, so the coach will challenge preconceptions and encourage their coachee to try out new ideas and behaviour, helping them to understand how they can learn from their experience. If we think of the sporting analogy, we can see that all coaching relies on practice and feedback, trying something different and developing what works.

Commitment to action

In coaching, as in all mentoring, something has to change. There has to be some sort of outcome. If the coachee is to commit to this successfully, they will need to be highly motivated, they will need appropriate support mechanisms, and some sort of review and evaluation to reinforce their new practice. Action plans should be S.M.A.R.T.E.R.:

- Specific
- Measurable
- Agreed

- Realistic
- Time-bound

And they should include some form of:

- Evaluation and
- Review.

Let's draw this process like we did the mentoring process:

The coaching process

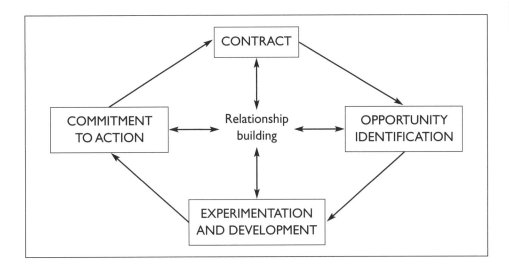

CONTRACT

COMMITMENT TO ACTION

Relationship building

OPPORTUNITY IDENTIFICATION

EXPERIMENTATION AND DEVELOPMENT

CLOSE FOCUS

1. Compare this to the mentoring diagram we drew in Chapter One. Where are the similarities?

2. Now look at the sorts of skills we've talked about in previous chapters. Which of these might also apply to coaching:

   - rapport-building;
   - listening;
   - questioning;
   - reflecting back;
   - summarising;
   - challenging;
   - reframing?

DISCUSSION

It was probably apparent from what we've said so far that all of the same sorts of skills apply to coaching as to other mentoring roles. Listening, questioning, summarising, challenging, reframing, etc. are crucial aspects of all one-to-one helping roles. We do not propose, therefore, to repeat what has already been said. A skill which we have so far touched upon very little, however, is giving feedback, so let us address that now.

Feedback – what not to do

At one time or another we've all been on the receiving end of badly delivered feedback. Positive feedback done badly can appear generalised and insincere, whilst poorly handled, negative feedback is a demotivating experience which undermines our self-esteem and dissipates any enthusiasm for further learning and growth.

TASK

Think about an occasion when you have been the victim of poorly handled feedback, and then read the following transcript of a coaching session between Benjamin and his mentor, Kate, to see if you can identify any similarities.

Kate and Benjamin – take one

Kate   Ah yes, come in, Benjamin. There's something we really need to talk about. That last workshop session of yours I observed was really not up to scratch.

Benjamin Is it alright if I sit down?

Kate   What? Oh yes, of course, of course. As I say, the workshop session was a bit of a disaster. Are you always that sloppy?

Benjamin Are we talking about the one three weeks ago? Because I've done a couple more since then that have gone a lot better.

Kate   Yes, but we're not talking about those. We're talking about the one I observed. You really can't afford to be that lackadaisical about your preparation and time management. Didn't you learn anything on your teaching practice?

Benjamin Well, that seems a bit harsh. I thought things settled down quite well after a while. The second half of the session really got the students talking. They might have been a bit boisterous, but they came up with some really good action points.

Kate	Look, Benjamin, I don't mean to give you a hard time. You seemed to get on well with the students and the session was, well, you know, very energetic...
Benjamin	But?
Kate	But you struck me as disorganised and a bit arty-farty, quite honestly. Perhaps if you dressed a bit more like a lecturer and a bit less like a student, they'd have more respect. Having said that, there's no doubt you were putting a lot of effort into it.
Benjamin	Thanks, but I think the students do respect me, actually. They seem less excitable when you're not there, watching. I suspect there was a bit of playing to the gallery.
Kate	You see, that's the trouble with you, Benjamin. You can't take criticism.

DISCUSSION

Was any of this familiar? Perhaps not. You may have suffered at the hands of 'everyone's mate', the person who never gives you any remotely critical feedback because he wants to stay friends with everyone. What feedback you do get is therefore, at best, vague and useless. Or perhaps you were under the wing of 'just get on with it'. She never gives any feedback, positive or negative, unless it's behind your back. You are expected to draw your own conclusions, a sort of learning by osmosis.

But where was Kate going wrong?

Poor feedback environment

There are certain conditions under which positive and negative feedback is more likely to be received constructively and without which all the good technique in the world may be wasted. We all know what these are from our own experience.

- Good rapport: if we are relaxed and at ease with someone it is easier to accept negative criticism and we take more notice of the positive. Feedback, like challenge, works best in an atmosphere of trust.
- Mutual respect: we obviously take more notice of those whom we feel are qualified to make observations, and we are more accepting of their observations if we think they respect us.
- Caring: it may sound a bit soppy, but knowing someone has your best interests and your development at heart makes a big difference to how their feedback comes across.
- Timeliness: we adults are no different from children in this regard, both praise and criticism are far more effective the closer they are to the event.

So did Kate make any effort to create this environment? Clearly not. She had waited far too long to discuss the feedback. She flung herself straight into her criticism, without any attempt at establishing some rapport or getting Benjamin relaxed. She showed him very little respect and did not seem to be on his side at all.

Expressing opinions

When we seek feedback we need descriptions, not opinions. What did we do right? What did we do wrong? What could we do differently? How can we respond to comments like

> *...you struck me as disorganised and a bit arty-farty, quite honestly. Perhaps if you dressed a bit more like a lecturer and a bit less like a student, they'd have more respect...*

without becoming defensive and demoralised?

Not being specific

In order to change and improve, in order to build on what we do well, we have to know exactly what it is we are doing which is effective and exactly what appears less successful. Wishy-washy statements which avoid the *reasons* why behaviour is positive or not are unhelpful. They are also usually the sign of someone who has not been paying close enough attention or has left their feedback too long.

> *That last workshop session of yours I observed was really not up to scratch.*

> *As I say, the workshop session was a bit of a disaster.*

Criticising the person not the performance

We can all change our behaviour, but it is a lot harder to change who we are. Getting personal just puts people on the defensive and undermines their self-esteem.

> *Are you always that sloppy?*

> *You really can't afford to be that lackadaisical about your preparation and time management.*

The particular danger here is that the person giving the feedback becomes victim to the 'halo' effect. In other words, they ascribe personal characteristics to the coachee which then subconsciously influence their whole perception of their performance.

Keeping it one-way

On the one occasion that Kate did ask a question, it was probably rhetorical. She made no effort to encourage self-reflection on Benjamin's part. We all know how much more committed we are to ideas that we have come up with ourselves, and how much less defensive we are about freely expressed self-criticism. Kate will never know how many of her observations are actually shared by Benjamin unless she asks him.

Misuse of the praise sandwich

Kate has clearly been on the course at some point, and rather late in the day she has a stab at the old 'good news–bad news–good news' approach. Unfortunately, handled badly this just means the recipient sees the 'but' coming a mile away and completely disregards any positive comments.

Kate *You seemed to get on well with the students and the session was, well, you know, very energetic.......*

Benjamin *But?*

Ignoring your own contribution

Very often the person giving feedback is in a position to contribute to the learner's success or failure by their own acts or omissions. As the boss, observer, or assessor we must be sensitive to how we might have affected the outcome we are describing. Benjamin may have a point when he alludes to this.

They seem less excitable when you're not there, watching.

Feedback – how to do it better

TASK

Look through the conversation between Kate and Benjamin again, and think about how you might have handled things differently in order to avoid some of the pitfalls we have just described.

Then compare your own thoughts with our suggestion as to how Kate could have done it better.

Kate and Benjamin – take two

Kate   *Hi there, Benjamin. Come in and have a seat. I'm just making some tea. Do you want one?*

Benjamin *Great, Kate, thanks. Just one sugar, please.*

Kate   *So how have these first few months gone? You finding your feet alright?*

Benjamin *Yes, I think so. I'm still struggling a bit to organise my time. I find things get a bit on top of me sometimes.*

►

71

Kate	Some of us have been at this years and still find that difficult, so don't give yourself too hard a time! Here's your tea. Perhaps we could talk about the organisation thing later? I might be able to help. I'd like to run through the workshop session I observed last Friday first though, if that's okay with you?
Benjamin	Yes, sure. How did I do?
Kate	Well I wanted to ask you first how you think you got on.
Benjamin	I thought it got people stimulated. It was a good lively session, with lots of debate. The group seemed pretty engaged. I suppose there were times, especially early on, when I didn't feel entirely in control of things.
Kate	Why do you think that might have been then?
Benjamin	I don't know. I thought I'd prepared enough. I did manage to get some good action points pulled together towards the end.
Kate	Okay let me say what I saw happening. I think you're absolutely right about the energy level. The way you presented the topic, using video clips, was a bit different and fun. The group was motivated to contribute and you did an excellent job of encouraging them, even the quieter ones. I felt a real buzz, and I was just observing. Towards the end you recognised that some proper outputs were needed. For example, you cleverly got Trevor, who was playing to the gallery a bit, to do the scribing and give you a chance to help the group draw conclusions. I suspect my being there may not help with the Trevors of this world, by the way.
	What about the middle bit though? I saw you get a bit caught up with arranging the brainstorm stuff and the group lost their way and all went off on different tangents. What do you think about that?
Benjamin	Yes, I know what you mean, but that's the problem with these sorts of session isn't it? You can't really prepare that much.
Kate	You've got to be flexible, true. But I felt a bit disappointed that things were allowed to drift. You would get marked down for that in an inspection. How could you have made what was a really lively and productive workshop feel even better run? Could you have prepared more carefully for how you were going to handle the brainstorm feedback?
Benjamin	I guess I could. Maybe I should have got one of the group to help as well, like I did at the end.
Kate	That would have been good. For me it was in essence a well-presented and creative workshop, which motivated the group, and which will benefit next time from us working on how you could smooth things out with more preparation. Let's look at that aspect now, shall we?

DISCUSSION

In this example Kate takes the time to let Benjamin settle down. She comes across as caring and supportive and she has arranged the feedback much closer to the event.

It is altogether a more two-way process, with Kate asking a lot of questions and encouraging Benjamin to assess his own performance. She steers clear of opinions and personal comments and sticks firmly to what she has observed, focusing on Benjamin's behaviour.

When she gives some feedback it is specific and accompanied by examples. She recognises where she may have contributed to Benjamin's difficulties herself, without letting him off the hook about his preparation. Instead of the formulaic 'feedback sandwich', Kate makes a balanced use of positive and negative feedback, and says how it makes her *feel*. Most importantly, she talks about what is at stake and the consequences of not improving performance, whilst showing a real resolve to help fix things. She also asks Benjamin for his response.

CLOSE FOCUS

Is there anything else that Kate could do to make her feedback more effective?

It starts with you

We have really only talked about giving feedback in this chapter, but there is a skill too in *receiving* feedback. Think about how well you respond to constructive criticism. One way to help people feel less defensive about feedback is to demonstrate that it is something good performers and experienced professionals know how to benefit from. If we subscribe to the idea of lifelong learning, then we seek out constructive feedback and continue to learn from it. Good mentors and coaches ask for feedback and respond positively to it. In this way they are also providing a role model for their mentees.

Summary – coaching and the dos and don'ts of feedback

As a mentor in FE we sometimes need to coach our mentees in order to help them improve their performance in specific areas. This can be seen as just another of the roles which a mentor is called upon to fulfil.

In coaching we follow a very similar process to mentoring in general, and use many of exactly the same skills to help an individual examine their experience, make sense of it and plan a way forward that contributes to their personal development.

More than in some other mentoring roles, coaching may require us to give feedback on a person's performance. There are some simple guidelines to remember if we are to do this effectively.

WHEN GIVING FEEDBACK DO	WHEN GIVING FEEDBACK DON'T
Be *prompt*, whether it is positive or negative.	Put it off, or avoid it altogether
Create the right *conditions*. As with all mentoring, it should take place in an atmosphere of trust and real rapport	Launch into a barrage of criticism in order to get it out of the way as quickly as possible
Ask *questions* to enable them to assess themselves first	Give them your opinions
Begin with two or three *positive things* which you want to praise	Be so general as to make it worthless
Follow with something that would make the performance even better next time	Criticise the individual on a personal level – stick to observations of behaviour and performance
Be *specific* – give examples and reasons	Be aloof
Don't be afraid to say how it makes you *feel* – good or bad	Interrupt
Be clear about what the consequences of not improving are	Brush over feelings
Recognise what contribution you may have made to any problems	Just think the 'praise sandwich' will do it for you!
Make clear your positive desire to *help resolve* any problems	
Ask for *their response* to what you have said	
Finish with an *overall positive comment*; consider getting them to summarise	

A final thought

Although dos and don'ts are fun, we suggest you focus on the dos. Another interesting observation about feedback is that our brains find it difficult to 'not do' something. If I ask you to not think of a red London bus, what happens?

When we give feedback therefore, it is always a good idea to phrase the improvements you agree upon positively. Stick to the dos.

Further reading

Landsberg, M (1996) *The Tao of Coaching*. London: HarperCollins.

Rogers, J (2001) *Adults Learning*. Buckingham: Open University Press (fourth edition).

Whitmore, J (2002) *Coaching for Performance*. London: Nicholas Brealey (third edition).

6. Mentoring yourself: the reflective mentor

CHAPTER OBJECTIVES

This chapter is designed to help you to:

- consider the important role that reflective practice plays in the development of effective mentoring;

- explore ways in which the mentor might reflect on their own performance in order to identify areas for further development;

- analyse ways in which reflection on practice might lead to improvement in the mentoring relationship as a whole;

- explore and critically apply relevant theory discussed in previous chapters.

Why reflect?

In Chapters One and Two we saw how one of the key functions of the mentor is to encourage the mentee to review and reflect on his or her professional practice, usually focusing on a specific lesson or incident or aspect of their role. In this instance the mentor's task is to help the mentee evaluate the quality of their own performance, to identify their current strengths and weaknesses, and to use this analysis in order to develop an action plan for the next step or stage in their professional development. And, of course, we've seen the various ways in which the mentor might do this: by asking pertinent and sometimes difficult questions, for example; or by modelling good practice against which the mentee can compare their own performance. But how might the mentor themselves go about reflecting on the effectiveness of their mentoring and the quality of the mentoring relationship?

Before we answer that, let's take a step back and address a more fundamental question which some of you may be asking yourselves: why is it necessary for the mentor to reflect on these things at all? After all, it's not really their professional development we're talking about, is it? As a matter of fact, it is, and probably the best way to explore this question is to have a look at a real-life example of mentoring in action.

TASK

The extract below is part of the feedback from a mentor to a student teacher following the mentor's observation of the student teacher's lesson. Here the mentor is fulfilling a coaching role (see Chapter Five). Read it through carefully and consider the following questions:

1. What skills does the student teacher need to work on?

2. What evidence is there here of the mentor reflecting on his *own* behaviour and practice?

Cert. Ed. Assessed teaching practice

Page 2. Assessing students' work and giving feedback

Brian, this was a difficult session because this particular group of adult learners are not very confident. You were just about okay at getting them into groups, making sure they understood the group task. But when it came to assessing them you clearly found yourself in difficulties. Don't you think you should have thought about this before you started? What's the point of setting an assessment task to a group and then trying to assess the students as individuals? It was obvious to me that you didn't know what you were doing, and I think it was pretty obvious to the learners, too. How are they going to have any confidence in your teaching now that they've seen how you can mess up? These adult learners – most of them returning to learning after a long break – feel nervous enough themselves without having to feel nervous for the teacher, too. Here are all the things you did wrong:

1. *You didn't think about the composition of the groups, so you ended up with all the able ones together and the other groups struggling to complete the task.*

2. *You set a group task and then tried to give individual feedback. What was that based on? How do you know who did what?*

3. *The way you gave feedback was terrible. It completely undermined what little confidence some of the learners had. You just told them everything they'd done wrong. Why couldn't you have found something they did well or at least not too badly, and given them a bit of praise?*

4. *And don't you think you'd inspire a bit more confidence if you smartened up a bit?*

DISCUSSION

I suppose if we were to take a charitable view of this we might suggest that maybe the mentor is trying to kick-start the student teacher's ability to empathise with these learners. One thing's for sure; the mentor leaves us in no doubt as to how we would answer that first question:

1. *What skills does the student teacher need to work on?* It's pretty clear that poor old Brian hasn't yet become very skilful at giving assessment feedback. He hasn't developed the knack of giving positive reinforcement. He's probably still at that early stage which most of us remember going through where he's concentrating so much on being a *teacher* that he's lost

sight of the *learning* end of the deal; that is, what his teaching feels like to somebody on the receiving end of it. There are other skills and strategies which you will have noted that Brian is struggling with, and we'll get on to those later, but let's consider our second question.

2. *What evidence is there here of the mentor reflecting on his own behaviour and practice?* You'll have noticed immediately, of course, that the mentor is displaying many of the same faults that he's criticising Brian for. His feedback to Brian about giving feedback in a destructive way is about as destructive as you could get! If this were simply a case of the pot calling the kettle black it would be bad enough, but what is probably more disturbing here is the mentor's apparent failure to recognise that he is doing this. He is criticising Brian in no uncertain terms for a weakness which he is not recognising, not acknowledging and not addressing in his own practice.

This is not, of course, to suggest that all mentors should be perfectly free from faults and weaknesses. If that were the case there would be nobody volunteering to fill the role. What it does highlight is that mentors need to have a certain level of self-knowledge, a realistic and – as far as possible – objective grasp of their own strengths and weaknesses. If they do not, they risk their advice coming over as less effective or even, as the example of Brian's mentor has shown, slightly ridiculous. The best way to achieve this understanding of their own strengths and weaknesses is through reflecting on their own performance as a mentor, as well as on their professional practice as a whole. A mentor also needs to reflect on their professional skills and practice in order to help their mentee make sense of their own experience. Imagine trying to teach someone to drive if you've never thought consciously about the skills and sequence of actions involved.

TASK

In Chapter Five we explored some of the skills required for giving effective feedback. Remind yourself, if necessary, of the key points and guidelines which are set out there and then look again at the written feedback to Brian from his mentor. How might you re-draft this in order to more effectively support Brian's professional development?

When you have drafted your version, compare it with the one we present below. Remember, there is not one perfect way of doing this; but if your version differs radically from ours you might like to discuss this with an interested colleague, or even with your mentor if you have one.

Cert. Ed. Assessed teaching practice

Page 2. Assessing students' work and giving feedback

Brian, this was a difficult session because this particular group of adult learners are not very confident. Lack of confidence is common amongst adult returners to education and training. I know I felt this way when I came back to college, and you'll recognise this too, no doubt, from your own experience of re-entering education after a gap of some years. It was a good idea of yours, therefore, to encourage them to work in groups, as this leaves individuals feeling less exposed. Perhaps another time you could consider assessing them and giving feedback to them as a group, too. This would solve two problems: a) you wouldn't be making them feel exposed as individuals at this early stage, and b) it's much easier to assess a group outcome of a group task. I think you recognised this last point when you began trying to give individual feedback, because it became clear to you that you couldn't know exactly who had contributed what. Perhaps you'd like to think about how you might handle this in a future session.

I've reflected a lot about this in my own classroom practice, and I'd suggest one useful tip for giving feedback. Try to find something positive to say, even if the student is getting it wrong, such as 'that's an interesting answer, but...' or 'thanks for having a go at that one, but...'. This sort of positive response won't scare them off trying to answer again on a future occasion.

To summarise, I think there are a couple of questions you might like to reflect on, and which we can pick up in our next meeting. First how to plan for the assessment of group tasks, and secondly how to give positive and encouraging feedback.

When we next meet I'd like to get your reaction to this feedback on what I've suggested here, and whether it's been helpful to you. Thank you for inviting me to observe the lesson.

One of the things you'll notice about this version is that it avoids the scattergun effect of criticising just about everything about Brian – including his dress sense. Instead it:

- picks up the key issues (group assessment and giving feedback);
- poses Brian a couple of key questions to think over;
- dispenses a bit of necessary wisdom (about adult returners);
- models good practice, not only in giving feedback and in professional courtesy, but also in setting an example of what it means to be a reflective practitioner.

DISCUSSION

A question that is immediately raised by the manner in which the first mentor expresses the feedback is, why doesn't he recognise that he's falling into the very same error that he's criticising the student teacher for? One answer to this might be found by considering for a moment what psychologists call *projection*. This is a term used to describe what happens when, instead of recognising a fault or area for development in ourselves, we become very good at recognising it in others. It is often the case that the more irritating we find this particular fault in others, the more blind we are to it in ourselves. We *project* it on to others, where we can safely disapprove of it while maintaining our own sense of self-righteousness. The giveaway in the case of Brian and the first mentor is the tone of irritation running through the feedback. Our own unacknowledged weaknesses infuriate us when we recognise them in others. In fact, that's often the first step in spotting what our hidden weaknesses are – those flaws we want to hide even from ourselves.

When we use terms like reflection and self-knowledge we are, among other things, talking about the ability and willingness to acknowledge and take back our projections; to be clear sighted about our own strengths and weaknesses; to be able to say to a mentee or other colleague, yes, *I have difficulty with that, too. And one of things I've found that helps is...* If you read again through those two mentor reports you'll see that both are pointing out the same areas for development, both are giving valuable advice. However, the second is much more likely than the other to inspire respect and trust, and to contribute towards the building of a productive and effective mentoring relationship because two essential features of the second mentor's report are self-disclosure and self-awareness:

> *Lack of confidence is common amongst adult returners to education and training. I know I felt this way when I came back to college.*

Increased self-awareness is one of the outcomes of careful reflection. This second mentor has quite clearly built reflection in as an essential component of her own practice as a professional educator:

> *I've reflected a lot about this in my own classroom practice.*

> *I'd like to get your reaction to this feedback on what I've suggested here, and whether it's been helpful to you.*

In other words, her approach is *do as I do.* This is very different from the first mentor, who gives no indication of reflection or self-awareness on a professional level. His so-called mentoring is ineffective – even destructive – for this very reason. After all, no one wants to hear about continuous learning from someone who feels they have nothing to learn themselves.

Reflecting on practice

So what strategies might that first mentor use in order to achieve greater self-knowledge and avoid sounding quite so much like Basil Fawlty? He might, for example, be persuaded to keep a mentoring journal. However, just jotting things down in a journal wouldn't necessarily get him very far, because in order to be effective in developing reflective practice it will be necessary for him to not only *describe* what he is doing as a mentor, but also to *evaluate* what he's doing and how he's doing it, and then go on to set out what he plans to do as a consequence. These three stages:

- describe;
- evaluate;
- plan;

are the key to successful reflective practice.

So let's assume we've persuaded him to sit down at his computer or his notebook and start reflecting on how his mentoring of Brian is coming along. What might his first page look like?

November 11th

Observed Brian today and gave him some written feedback. He messed up the assessment, setting them a group task and then trying to assess them individually without having any idea of who contributed what. And then he goes and gives them totally negative feedback, nothing but criticism, completely destroying what little confidence they have. What a prat. And I told him so. He's going to have to improve on this, or he's just wasting his time and mine.

He's made a start here by *describing* what has happened. Now let's assume he has a think about it and writes a bit more:

When I gave him the feedback to read he looked a bit upset. In fact, he looked very upset and cut our conversation short and left. But he's not going to get anywhere in this game if he can't take criticism.

So he's noticed that Brian reacted badly to the feedback. However, instead of reflecting on his own behaviour the mentor is still focusing on finding deficiencies in Brian's. According to this way of thinking, Brian is upset because 'he can't take it'. In this way the mentor is still protecting himself from recognising his own poor practice. But what if Brian does the sensible thing and comes back and explains how he's feeling?

Nov 12th

Got in this morning and there was Brian waiting for me. He'd brought the feedback sheet with him and said he wanted to go over it with me. He said he didn't think it was fair, me criticising him when he's modelling what he does on how I do it. He said that I'm snappy and abrupt with learners when they give the wrong answers, and I never praise anybody, and if I want proof just look at how I've written the feedback for him. And so why should he get criticised for doing it my way? He thought that was the whole idea – to watch his mentor and learn how things were done.

This was very awkward. I ended up apologising if I'd expressed the feedback too harshly, but made it clear that the criticisms I made still stand. He went off then, still not looking very happy. Thing is, he may be right, in a way. I don't think I do hand out praise very easily. Not that there's much to praise with some of the learners I get these days. I've obviously upset Brian, and he's not a bad bloke really. At least he had the guts to tell me how he felt. I don't think some of the young learners would do that – so I guess it's possible that my manner could be seen as a bit discouraging without me knowing it, because there's been nobody who dares tell me so. And when I read through this feedback I wrote for Brian it does come over as a bit of a rant.

Here we see the mentor begin to *evaluate* his behaviour in this particular instance and, by extension, to critically review his usual practice. He has now achieved the second stage in the reflective process. What he needs to do next is to use what he's learned from this in order to plan for future practice.

Nov 13th

Having slept on it, I think I'm going to have to admit that Brian's right. I maybe owe him a more genuine apology. And I think we'd better fix another meeting asap to help him identify his strengths as well as his weaknesses. And I've got the Year 2s today and I'm going to make a conscious effort to find something positive to say, and to avoid biting their heads off when they get things wrong. And let's face it, they get things wrong most of the time – but then it looks like I'm not always perfect either, so there you go.

Bingo! This mentor is on his way to becoming a reflective practitioner. He's now allowing himself not just to describe, but also to evaluate and learn from this incident in order to make an action plan for future practice. Of course, it's not always as easy as this. An unreflective professional with an 'I'm always right' attitude is rarely so quickly converted, whatever their role within the organisation. And in reality it's unlikely (one would hope) that someone with such obvious blind spots about their own strengths and weaknesses would be asked to step into the role of mentor, or, having taken on the role, would be allowed to remain in it for very long. Brian's first mentor is clearly a caricature, but not so much so that we don't recognise some elements of his mindset in ourselves or in colleagues we have encountered.

Reflection as an aspect of professionalism

In Chapter Seven we'll be looking at how the effectiveness of mentoring may be evaluated on an institutional, programme and individual level; in other words how systems of objective, systematic monitoring may operate. What it is important to remember, however, is that the reflective mentor is *evaluating their own effectiveness* on an ongoing basis: a subjective, reflective monitoring. Given the increasingly high profile that mentoring now plays in professional development for FE (as we saw in the Introduction), it is of crucial importance that the mentor's support of the mentee is both structured and effective. Reflective practice – an ability and willingness to evaluate our own effectiveness and make changes to our practice where necessary – is an important aspect of professionalism. Indeed, it would be possible to argue that it is this self-monitoring and evaluation that is at the very heart of what we mean by 'being a professional'.

TASK

Below you will find three examples of mentors talking about mentoring. Read them through carefully, making notes if necessary, and consider the following questions.

- Which of these mentors, if any, are thinking reflectively about their mentoring?

- Can you identify any examples in what they say of the reflective process discussed earlier in this chapter: describe, evaluate, plan?

- If you were Anne's line manager, what feedback or advice would you give her about her mentoring role?

A. Telephone conversation between Cert Ed course leader and subject mentor, Anne.

CL	So how's she getting on?
Anne	Jasmine? Well, I'm sorry to say it, but I've got a lot of concerns about her.
CL	Really? I'm surprised you say that.
Anne	Why surprised?
CL	Just that when I saw her teach last week I was quite pleased with her.
Anne	Oh, her teaching's alright. It's her attitude that bothers me.
CL	Her attitude?
Anne	She's too friendly with the students. She goes off to the refectory with them at break; she's always laughing and carrying on with them.
CL	Carrying on? Oh.
Anne	No, no. I mean she jokes with them and chatters on with them and doesn't take anything seriously. She just wants them to like her, and I expect they do. I expect they like her more than me. I expect they'd rather have her teaching them than me. Well, that's fine. But that's not what it's all about, is it? It's not about being friends with them. It's about …
CL	But are the students learning, do you think? Is she being effective at teaching and supporting learning? Are they meeting outcomes and all the rest of it?
Anne	Oh yes, yes, they're meeting outcomes alright. It's just her attitude that bothers me.
CL	You feel she's not behaving professionally? Is that it?
Anne	That's exactly it. Not behaving professionally. Yes.
CL	So have you addressed this with her?
Anne	Yes I have. I said to her, 'Jasmine, look, this is no way to carry on. You're getting too pally with them. You need to back off a bit.' And she says, 'Why? What for? It's nice. They learn better when they feel it's a nice atmosphere. I like them; they like me. There's no harm in it.' And so I say, 'What do you mean, they learn better? Better than with me, you mean?' And she goes, 'No. Well, yes. But I'm not getting at you, Anne.' And so I walked off. You can't tell her anything. She's here to learn from me, and there she is, trying to tell me she can do it better. Well, that sort of attitude isn't going to get her anywhere, I'm afraid.
CL	Have you spoken to her since?
Anne	What's the point? She doesn't seem to think she needs my advice.
CL	Well, you know, Anne, she always speaks very highly of you to me. I think she really values the help and support you've given her. It may just be that she's developing a teaching style that's slightly different from yours. And that's a great credit to you, that you've given her the confidence and the enthusiasm to develop her own style. Don't you think?
Anne	Well, I don't know about that.
CL	And I would imagine students benefit from experiencing a range of teaching styles, wouldn't you?
Anne	I wouldn't call it a teaching style. I'd call it ingratiating herself with the students. She wants them to like her best. And she thinks she knows everything. She's even had the cheek to leave a book on my desk.
CL	Schon's 'The Reflective Practitioner'?
Anne	Never heard of it. No. This one's by somebody called Carl Rogers.

DISCUSSION: REFRAMING

One of the things that this conversation illustrates is that constructive dialogue also has the potential to act as a vehicle for reflection. In this particular instance, as you'll have noticed, it resoundingly fails; but not without the course leader doing his best to encourage Anne to see her concerns in a different light. This seeing things in a different light is sometimes referred to as reframing, as we saw in Chapter Four. By encouraging someone to reframe an issue we can sometimes help them to get a different, more helpful perspective on it. Reframing can be an essential element of reflective practice. So let's look again at how the course leader tries to encourage this strategy.

1. He identifies the way in which Anne is currently framing this issue:

   I expect they like her more than me. I expect they'd rather have her teaching them than have me.

   It's clear from what Anne says that this is her main concern, and that this insecurity is colouring her perception of the whole issue. She describes Jasmine's behaviour as unprofessional, but what in fact she is seeing is a threat to her own status, her authority and her self-esteem; and she finds it impossible to see past this to the key facts which are apparent from this dialogue:

   - Jasmine is succeeding as a teacher (*Oh, her teaching's alright...Oh yes, yes, they're meeting outcomes*);
   - Anne herself deserves some credit for this;
   - Jasmine has no malign intent to undermine her.

2. He suggests another way of looking at it, in which both Jasmine and Anne can be seen to be successful in their respective roles of student teacher and mentor:

   It may just be that she's developing a teaching style that's slightly different from yours. And that's a great credit to you, that you've given her the confidence and the enthusiasm to develop her own style.

   But this fails in this instance to help Anne to see past her own insecurities:

   I'd call it ingratiating herself with the students. She wants them to like her best. And she thinks she knows everything.

   Just as we saw that Brian's mentor's inability to reflect usefully was caused by a tendency to resort to projection, so Anne's inability must be attributed here to a sense of insecurity. In both cases a lack of clarity about their own feelings and thought processes is getting in the way of these mentors doing their job properly. One brief telephone conversation was clearly not enough to get Anne reflecting on how her own feelings were obscuring the facts of the situation. It's interesting, however, to see the course leader having a go at mentoring the mentor!

CLOSE FOCUS

1. The book that Jasmine left on Anne's desk was by Carl Rogers. What do you think was the significance of that?

2. There was at least one opportunity in that conversation for the course leader to gain a better understanding of where Anne was coming from, and thereby perhaps help her more effectively to start questioning her own assumptions. This opportunity was missed. Did you spot it? Anne says:

> But that's not what it's all about, is it? It's not about being friends with them. It's about...

But here the course leader cuts her off, just as she's about to articulate what, for her, lies at the heart of teaching and supporting learning. That's the sort of mistake an effective mentor would always try to avoid. Wouldn't you?

If you had been that course leader, what sort of questions might you have asked of Anne in order to prompt her to reflect on some of her assumptions?

B. Discussion between Mo, a recently appointed team leader, and Raquelle, who is an experienced team leader and is mentoring him in his new role.

R Okay, Mo. What I think we should talk about this week is...

M Hang on. Listen. I'm having a bit of a problem with Tony and one of the learning support assistants. Could we just...?

R Mo, I'm so sorry. There I go again, wanting to set the agenda without finding out what issues have come up for you this week.

M No problem.

R No, no. It is a problem. I really must watch myself on that one. Anyway, go on. A problem with Tony?

M And one of the learning support assistants. Yes. Apparently this chap – he's there to support one of Tony's basic skills group – keeps getting nasty with the class; telling them to shut up; jeering at them when they get things wrong; generally throwing his weight about. Tony reckons it's undoing all the good work he's put in. He wants him out.

R And he wants you to do it?

M Yep.

R Lucky you. So how are you going to go about it?

M I don't know. How am I going to go about it? You tell me.

R Listen, Mo. You know there's nothing I like better than jumping in and telling people how to do things. And I think I probably do it far too often – I can see you smiling so I know it's true. The thing is, I don't think that's quite what mentoring's about. You're not going to gain confidence that way. So come on. Let's hear how you think you might handle this. And then we'll discuss what I would do, if you still want to hear it.

M I think I like it better when you just tell me.

R Well, let's call this the new approach. Otherwise I'm going to be learning more from this mentoring arrangement than you have.

DISCUSSION

It's clear from the outset that this mentor is willing and able to take an objective look at her own practice. We catch her reflecting out loud here, catching herself in the act of being too directive and changing her approach accordingly. She's not only prepared to point out her own weaknesses, but doesn't hesitate to apologise for them. She's a good illustration of our assertion that an effective mentor doesn't have to be perfect as long as they're able to look critically and analytically at how they carry out their mentoring role. By voicing that critical analysis out loud, Raquelle is here providing a good role model for Mo. She's illustrating for him a) how it's done, and b) that it's okay to do it and it's not an expression of weakness or failure.

We can identify the model of reflection here quite clearly.

- Describe: *there I go again, wanting to set the agenda without finding out what issues have come up for you this week.*
- Analyse: *it is a problem...You're not going to gain confidence that way.*
- Plan: *I really must watch myself on that one.*

And:

- Describe: *there's nothing I like better than jumping in and telling people how to do things.*
- Evaluate: *I think I probably do it far too often... I don't think that's entirely what mentoring's about.*
- Plan: *let's hear how you think you might handle this.*

CLOSE FOCUS

1. Mo says, perhaps jokingly, that he prefers to be told what to do. There is no doubt that some colleagues would genuinely prefer this. However, could we then legitimately call what would be happening mentoring? If you're not sure how to answer this, you might like to look again in Chapter One where we discuss the distinctions between mentoring and other supportive roles.

2. Raquelle says it would be better if she resists telling Mo what to do all the time, *Otherwise, I'm going to be learning more from this mentoring arrangement than you have.* Can you think of any examples from this or previous chapters, or from your own experience, where the mentor appears to be learning more than the mentee? In your view does this invalidate the mentoring arrangement? You may like to discuss this question with an interested colleague, or with your mentor if you have one.

C. An extract from a mentor's journal

Jan 22nd

Exhausting meeting with Winnie today. She really does feel the world's against her. This makes it almost impossible to get her to think critically about her teaching, because she reacts defensively every time I try to raise an issue. She's been teaching here so long now that I suppose she sees it as an attack on her professional status that she's been allocated a mentor at all, let alone someone like me – half her age and with half her years of experience. This is why I have to tread sensitively. Things have moved on and changed so much since Winnie started teaching here, and widening participation has brought in learners with characteristics that she's never really encountered before in the classroom: confrontational behaviour, low levels of literacy and other basic skills, and a disaffection about education – which shows up as a distrust of all teachers. She was insulated from all that, Winnie was, over there in the old Sixth Form College. So now she's struggling. And when I tried to talk to her today about the need for different teaching styles for learners who don't know how to make notes and can't concentrate for long, she just took it as a personal attack again. She only seems to understand praise on the one hand or criticism on the other. She doesn't see yet that's there's middle ground, a neutral place, that's to do with having a careful look at what's actually going on and seeing if there's need for change.

So I've got to find some way to reassure her and get her thinking about ways of extending her range of teaching and classroom management skills. And at the same time I have to get around this problem that she finds it humiliating to be offered help and support by me. I was thinking about this a lot while I was driving over to the annexe to take the evening class – because I don't want to be dreading every meeting with Winnie; and I don't want her to be dreading them either. And so I think what I might try is asking her if we can do some team teaching. I'll tell her I've got a big group – the 2nd years'll do – and could do with some help and in return I'll come in and lend a hand with one of her classes. Have to see whether the timetable will allow this. But if it does it might just work, because she'll have a chance to see how I do things, but under the pretext that she's helping me out. And if we team teach one or two of her classes (in the guise of me repaying the favour), I may be able to demonstrate some strategies there too that'll work for her. I reckon it's worth a try, anyway.

DISCUSSION

Just because a mentor is keeping a Journal about their mentoring role, it doesn't necessary follow that they are reflecting on and learning from their experience of this aspect of their professional practice. In the extract from this mentor's journal, however, the reflective model – with which we are now familiar – is clearly identifiable.

- Describe: *when I tried to talk to her today about the need for different teaching styles for learners who don't know how to make notes and can't concentrate for long, she just took it as a personal attack.*
- Analyse/evaluate: *She's been teaching here so long now that I suppose she sees it as an attack on her professional status that she's been allocated a mentor at all.*
- Plan: *I think what I might try is asking her if we can do some team teaching.*

You'll notice here that these three stages don't have to be written down exactly in that order. This mentor has presumably done his or her thinking in that logical sequence; and then, in writing it down, they've given us their analysis of the situation before describing exactly what happened that day. The reflection is a thought process that has later been recorded on the page. It's worth reminding ourselves here that:

- reflection does not always throw up ideas that work;
- there's no guarantee that every problem can be successfully addressed through reflective practice.

CLOSE FOCUS

As a matter of interest, and on reflection, do you think this mentor's solution is likely to work? If so, why? If not, why not? You might find it interesting to share views on this with an interested colleague or with your own mentor, if you have one.

Summary

In this chapter we have looked at the how and the why of reflective mentoring. We've seen that the process is an ongoing one and that it hinges on the same model of reflective action planning that we discussed in Chapter One as one we would wish to encourage in our mentees: describe, evaluate, plan, describe and so on. We have seen examples of reflection being facilitated by keeping a journal, by conversations with others, or simply by thinking out loud. We have also seen that one key purpose of reflective practice is to help us arrive at a level of self-knowledge where we can recognise our projections and our fears sufficiently well to avoid them presenting a barrier to effective mentoring. In other words, this chapter has been about how we, in our role as mentor, can monitor and evaluate our own effectiveness. In the chapter that follows we shall explore some of the ways in which a more formal evaluation of mentor effectiveness may be achieved, both on the institutional and the individual level.

References and further reading

Rogers, C (1983) *Freedom to Learn for the 80s*. Columbus, OH: Merrill.

Schon, Donald A (1985) *The Reflective Practitioner: How professionals think in action*. New York: Basic Books.

Wallace, S (2007) *Teaching, Tutoring and Training in the Lifelong Learning Sector* (3rd edition) Exeter: Learning Matters.

7. Effective mentor = Effective teacher?

> ## CHAPTER OBJECTIVES
>
> This chapter is designed to help you to:
>
> - consider the importance of monitoring and evaluation both in supporting individual mentors and in sustaining a system of effective mentoring;
>
> - consider ways in which mentors themselves can be supported and how their mentoring role can be made to serve their own professional development as well as the development of the college or organisation as a whole;
>
> - explore ways in which the skills of mentoring are reflected in good classroom practice;
>
> - explore the ways in which mentoring – as well as teaching – can contribute to creating a learning organisation;
>
> - explore and critically apply relevant theory discussed in previous chapters.

Why evaluate?

One of the reasons we need to evaluate our mentoring is for exactly the same purpose that we need to evaluate our teaching; that is, to discover whether it is working. In order to discover whether it's working, we have to have a clear idea of what the mentoring is setting out to do, just as we have to be clear – by setting out our learning objectives – about what a particular programme of teaching is setting out to do. Unless we're clear about the purpose, we will find any individual example or organised scheme of mentoring impossible to evaluate.

Let's start this chapter by having a look at an example of mentoring which you'll probably recognise.

The Dodger made a sudden stop and laying his finger on his lip, drew his companions back again, with the greatest caution and circumspection.

'What's the matter?' demanded Oliver.

'Hush!' replied the Dodger. 'Do you see that old cove at the bookstall?'

'The old gentleman over the way?' said Oliver. 'Yes, I see him.'

'He'll do,' said the Dodger.

'A prime plant,' observed Master Charley Bates.

Oliver looked from one to the other, with the greatest surprise; but he was not permitted to make any enquiries, for the two boys walked stealthily across the road, and slunk close behind the old gentleman towards whom his attention had been directed. Oliver walked a few paces after them, and, not knowing whether to advance or retire, stood looking on in silent amazement.

> What was Oliver's horror and alarm as he stood a few paces off, looking on with eyelids as wide open as they would possibly go, to see the Dodger plunge his hand into the old gentleman's pocket, and draw from thence a handkerchief! To see him hand the same to Charley Bates, and finally to behold them, both, running away round the corner at full speed.
>
> In an instant the whole mystery of the handkerchiefs, and the watches, and the jewels rushed upon the boy's mind. He stood for a moment, then, confused and frightened, he took to his heels, and, not knowing what he did, made off as fast as he could lay his feet to the ground. In the very instant when Oliver began to run, the old gentleman, putting his hand to his pocket and missing his handkerchief, turned sharp round. Seeing the boy scudding away at such a rapid pace, he very naturally concluded him to be the depredator, and, shouting 'Stop thief!' with all his might, made off after him.

And of course this sorry tale of mentoring gone wrong results in Oliver Twist being arrested for a crime he didn't commit. No such dire consequence is likely to follow from any mentoring you or I are involved with – at least, we hope not. But this well-known story will help us to identify some key points about the whys and hows of evaluating a mentoring system or situation. The Victorians were rather fond of holding up disastrous examples to make a pedagogic point, so Dickens will serve our purpose nicely here. In the case of Oliver and the Dodger, we're considering the evaluation of mentoring on a relationship level. There is, of course, a clear distinction between this and evaluation at an organisational level, which we shall be moving on to later in this chapter.

First let's apply the question that we identified as our starting point: What was the objective of this mentoring? What was it setting out to achieve? The answer to this is pretty clear. Oliver was to watch and learn from the Dodger's example of how best to a) identify a likely target; b) surreptitiously pick his pocket; and c) run away. So far so good. But there's an essential element missing here. Did you spot it?

> Oliver looked from one to the other, with the greatest surprise; but he was not permitted to make any enquiries.

Exactly! The objective of the exercise might be clear to the Dodger, but Oliver himself has no idea what's going on. So if we were to ask him to evaluate his experience of being mentored, he'd have no criteria on which to base a response. He might be able to tell us that the Dodger is an affable sort of geezer, but that wouldn't get us very far.

So now we have two prerequisites for the effective evaluation of mentoring:

1. Have clear objectives.
2. Make sure both the mentor and the mentee know what these are.

We've discussed in previous chapters the importance of mentor and mentee setting the agenda. This may be where the objectives are set, reviewed and revised as the mentoring progresses. If this is happening, then the danger of one party or the other being unclear about the objectives can be avoided. However, it's often the case in FE when a system of mentoring is put in place – whether for supporting trainee teachers or for raising college-wide standards of leadership or classroom practice – that a set of common objectives applies, in addition to those specific to the individual mentee. In the case of Oliver it was presumably Fagin – the pickpockets' 'Mr Big' – who had imposed the objective for Dodger's mentoring of Oliver. The equivalent Mr or Ms Big in FE might be the college's senior management team; or an external body such as the LSC or Ofsted; or a partnership organisation such as a university which provides validation for PGCE or Cert Ed programmes. Any of these might require certain outcomes from the mentoring process, and it is essential that both mentor and mentee are familiar with these.

Oliver can't evaluate this example of mentoring because he didn't know what was going on; and the Dodger can't evaluate it because he's run away. So let's have a go at evaluating it ourselves, from an objective viewpoint, without the benefit of feedback from those actually involved.

In terms of the objective – turning Oliver into a proficient pickpocket – the mentoring is evidently a failure. We can list some of the reasons for this:

- the mentee doesn't know what it is he's supposed to be learning;
- the mentee is given no opportunity for asking questions;
- the mentor employs jargon that the mentee isn't familiar with;
- the mentor makes no concessions to the mentee's lack of knowledge and experience.

And so on. The consequence of this – that Oliver as mentee suffers unjustly because of a failure in mentoring, while his mentor happily gets away with it – is a vivid reminder of why the evaluation of mentoring is so important. Similarly there's a lesson to be learned here from the fact that the Dodger's evident skill as a pickpocket doesn't in itself make him a useful mentor. It reminds us, if we once again need reminding, that there's more to mentoring than is involved in what factory workers used to call 'sitting next to Nelly'.

CLOSE FOCUS

We have been able to make an evaluation here without benefit of feedback from either mentor or mentee. But what might we be missing in such a case? What might Oliver's or the Dodger's viewpoint have usefully added to the evaluation?

DISCUSSION

You have probably concluded that feedback from the mentor and mentee might have thrown light on some of the following.

- Whether the Dodger had received any mentor preparation or training.
- Whether the Dodger has a realistic view of his mentoring skills and strategy.

- How Oliver feels about being mentored by the Dodger.
- Whether the mentoring relationship is working positively in ways that aren't immediately obvious to us; for example, building Oliver's confidence or self-esteem; giving him space to reflect.

This kind of feedback is invaluable because it goes beyond what we can simply observe as evaluators looking from outside the mentoring relationship. Observation will usually tell us whether the mentoring is working or not; but it won't necessarily show us the underlying reasons for success or failure.

We are now in a position, therefore, to add a third prerequisite for effective evaluation.

1. Have clear objectives.
2. Make sure both the mentor and the mentee know what these are.
3. Elicit evaluative feedback from the mentor and mentee.

So we now have a sequence that looks something like this:

Objectives

|

Observation and feedback

|

Evaluation

The evaluation process

This simple sequence, however, has one big drawback. Let's assume, in the case of Oliver and the Dodger, that the person with a vested interest in evaluating the success or otherwise of the mentoring is Fagin, the Mr Big or *übermentor* of the pickpockets. It would seem from the account we've just read that the first he's going to know about how things are shaping up is that it's all a complete disaster and Olivier has picked up none of the requisite skills and knowledge from the Dodger – not even the basic skill of running away on cue. This evaluation is going to be too little too late: no feedback from the key people involved, and no opportunity for an intervention to get the mentoring on a firmer footing. In other words, what was missing here was any kind of ongoing monitoring. Now this, as it happens, was probably quite lucky for Oliver, whose story would have had a very different ending if successful mentoring had turned him into just another pickpocket. But for professionals in education the monitoring of any mentoring arrangement is essential if evaluation is to be used in order to support and improve existing practice. *Eliciting feedback at the end of mentoring – whether in relation to a single relationship or an entire scheme – is too late.*

So now we have another precondition for effective evaluation and that is that we have to have some system for monitoring, so that we're getting formative feedback about what's going on. Our list now looks like this.

1. Have clear objectives.
2. Make sure both the mentor/s and the mentee/s know what these are.
3. Elicit evaluative feedback from the mentor/s and mentee/s, both summative (at the end) and formative (ongoing).
4. Establish a system of systematic monitoring.

In terms of a flow chart, these steps would look like this:

Objectives
|
Monitoring: formative observation and feedback
|
Summative observation and feedback
|
Evaluation

But in order to make it clear that the purpose of evaluation, like any other quality assurance exercise, is to feed back into and improve practice, it makes better sense to present the process like this:

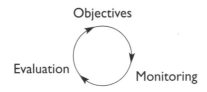

Objectives

Evaluation

Monitoring

Once again we come back to that essential, cyclical process of setting objectives, acting on them, monitoring progress, evaluating progress, and then – if necessary – reviewing and/or revising our objectives. As we've discussed in earlier chapters, this process can be usefully applied on a number of levels: to the mentoring process and relationship itself; to mentees' reflection on their professional development; to mentors' reflection on their own mentoring experience and practices; and now – as we see – to the systematic evaluation of a particular example, or indeed an institutional system, of mentoring. The cyclical evaluative process allows for intervention at any point in order to keep the process a) on track and b) relevant to the developmental needs of the mentee. As we shall see from one of the case studies that follows, it can be argued that evaluation and monitoring should start in the early stages as well as happening part-way through and again at the end.

Evaluating a scheme of mentoring

Evaluation can have wider purposes than discovering whether an individual mentoring relationship is working. These purposes are likely to be institutional ones. They may include the following.

- Assessing and assuring the quality of all institutional systems and processes for the purposes of continuous improvement.
- Assessing and assuring the overall quality of specific programmes of staff development and training.

- Meeting institutional goals for the professional development of human resources.
- Institutional aspirations towards continuous learning.
- Monitoring to ensure no undesirable legal or ethical issues arise.
- Gathering data which will support positive feedback to participants.
- Gathering data which will provide evidence to senior management of value for money.

Such evaluation on a programme-wide or an institution-wide scale will usually, as we shall see, demand a wider range of monitoring and evaluation strategies, appropriate for application on a wider scale, than those necessary for the evaluation of individual mentoring relationships.

We've spent long enough now in Dickensian London with disaffected youngsters, so let's get back to Further Education in the twenty-first century (okay, so there might still be some disaffected youngsters about) and apply some of what we've learned to a scenario we'll all be fairly familiar with: the system of mentoring trainee teachers on a PGCE/Cert Ed (FE) programme. In previous chapters we've encountered various examples of feedback about their mentoring experience from both mentors and mentees. Some have raised problems, but many have been very positive. They have all, however, been separate snapshots of individual examples of mentoring. What we're going to look at now is some evaluative feedback from a number of mentors and their mentees involved in one particular teacher training programme. The mentors are all experienced teachers who have been asked to support the subject knowledge and develop the teaching skills of their mentees. The mentees are all full-time PGCE/Cert Ed students on a college-taught programme validated by a local university. They have all been asked by the PGCE programme leader at college to give evaluative feedback ten weeks into the ten-month programme. The questions they were asked were: how is your mentoring progressing? Do you have any problems or questions?

TASK

Most of the responses were positive and reassuring. What we've picked out here, however, are some of the more 'interesting' ones. Read through the following examples of what they have to say and consider the following questions:

- What are the key issues you would identify from this feedback?
- What interventions might you want to make?
- What other methods of evaluation could have been introduced here?
- If you were to follow up this initial feedback with a questionnaire, what questions would you want to ask?
- In reviewing the mentoring programme, what changes might you want to make for the following year?
- If you were to follow up this monitoring exercise by putting together a development programme for mentors, what would you put on the agenda?

RESPONSES FROM MENTORS	RESPONSES FROM MENTEES
Jo *It's going fine. Darren is doing very well. He's been sitting in on a lot of my classes and then discussing what he's seen with me afterwards. I've given him small groups to work with, which has gone well. And this week he's taken a whole class for the first time. The students like him, and he gets on well with all the staff here. We have regular meetings to discuss and update his action plan. The only question I have is: do I get paid for this?*	Darren *Jo's really nice and she's helped me to settle in here. She's always happy to answer questions and let me talk things through with her, and she gives me a lot of time, like with regular meetings for the action plan. I'm a bit worried that she always says everything's fine, though. I'd quite like to know what I could improve on, but my action plan points always come from me. Question: How do I know if I'm really doing well, or if she's just being kind?*
Lenny *As far as I can see, everything's going well. Par's doing great. We started off with her shadowing me and asking questions, then taking bits of a lesson now and again. Now she's filling in for one of our team who's off sick and she's managing nearly a full teaching timetable. Question: Can we have someone as good as this next year?*	Parveen *My mentor's nice and has a great sense of humour, but I don't see him much now because I'm doing cover for someone and I don't have time to think really. I'm a bit worried about having all this responsibility. One question I've got is, can I extend the hand-in date for my coursework? I've got so much teaching, I can't get it finished.*
Gill *No problems. I'm about to take on an additional role here as head of mentoring. If you'd like me to come and talk to your new mentors about how to do successful mentoring I'd be happy to do so.*	Ollie *I don't see much of my mentor, she's really busy, and I feel like I'm being a nuisance if I try to ask her something. She says to make an appointment to see her, but then she doesn't turn up. I know it's because she's so busy, running the department and everything, but I feel a bit lost really. Not sure I can cope with this. Question: Can I talk to you about maybe dropping out until next year?*
Raj *Brenda and I have been through the Mentor Handbook and the PGCE Student Handbook and made sure we know what we're supposed to be doing, and when. This took some time, but we both felt it was worth it. We're up to date on the checklist, i.e. Brenda's done shadowing, observation of me, teaching small groups, and now she's taken two of my classes, with me sitting in for support. We have twice-weekly meetings to talk about her action plan and to reflect on her practice – and mine. And I must tell you, I think I'm learning as much from this as she is! Very time-consuming, but a rewarding experience. Only one question: What's the maximum number of hours she should be teaching per week? I don't want to overload her at this stage.*	Brenda *Having Raj as a mentor is one of the best bits about this course. I think I'm really lucky. When I don't understand something I know I can always ask him – and if he doesn't understand something – like about the course – he asks me. I know some other people on the course don't feel very happy with their mentors, and I suppose my only question is: isn't it a bit unfair that I get such a good mentor and other people get rubbish ones? Shouldn't you make sure they're all doing it properly?*

▶

RESPONSES FROM MENTORS	RESPONSES FROM MENTEES
Lynette *How is the mentoring progressing? I'm not sure what this question means.*	Pansy *My mentor has no idea. She's perfectly nice, but she clearly hasn't even read the Mentor's Handbook. In fact she denies ever having been given one, and I know she's had one because I put it into her hands myself. She also says she never volunteered to do it, she was just told she was going to be a mentor, end of story. When I asked to see her lesson plans she told me she doesn't bother doing any. In fact she says nobody bothers with that – which is patently not true. Her lessons are rubbish, the students come and go and disrespect her and she does nothing about it. She's just crap, basically. So my question is: What are you going to do about it?*

Discussion

What are the key issues you would identify from this feedback? The issues you noted down are likely to have included some of the following.

Jo and Darren	*...she always says everything's fine, though. I'd quite like to know what I could improve on, but my action plan points always come from me.*
	Jo seems to be very good at giving positive feedback and encouragement, but Darren's comment suggests that she lacks the confidence or skills to draw Darren's attention to points for development.
Lenny and Parveen	*...she's filling in for one of our team who's off sick and she's managing nearly a full teaching timetable.*
	This is clearly not satisfactory. Parveen is in college to learn, not to solve a staffing crisis. Lenny's failure to prevent Parveen from being exploited in this way suggests that the aims and objectives of the mentored teaching practice placement are not clear to him.
Gill and Ollie	*I feel like I'm being a nuisance if I try to ask her something. She says to make an appointment to see her, but then she doesn't turn up.*
	Ollie's comment on his mentor will send us immediate alarm signals, which are compounded when we read the blithely unselfcritical feedback from Gill (remember the Johari Window?). The issue here goes deeper than that of simply matching a mentee with a suitable mentor. This mentor wouldn't suit anybody. How did she come to be selected? Perhaps she volunteered with an eye to her career. The issue here is about recruitment and selection.

Raj and Brenda	*Isn't it a bit unfair that I get such a good mentor and other people get rubbish ones? Shouldn't you make sure they're all doing it properly?*
	Absolutely! This is the key issue here, and one which is heavily emphasised by Ofsted as an important issue on such programmes nationally.
	And: *What's the maximum number of hours she should be teaching per week? I don't want to overload her at this stage.*
	If a conscientious mentor like Raj is asking this question, we have to assume that there's a communication problem somewhere resulting in him receiving insufficient information.
Lynette and Pansy	*My mentor has no idea.*
	Where to start? It isn't simply that Lynette doesn't know what her role as mentor entails. It's also that she has made no effort to find out. Saying she hasn't seen the Mentor Handbook is one way of getting out of reading it. But it's not just that she's not fulfilling her role; she's actually behaving in a counter-productive way, advising her mentee against writing lesson plans, for example. The issue here again is about recruitment and selection; and perhaps also mentor training. And, as in the case of Ollie's mentor Gill, we may also have an issue here about monitoring. Ten weeks into the placement, it's rather late to be picking up disastrous cases like this.

Clearly, some of the feedback we're getting here raises the question of confidentiality. Some quite serious allegations and damning comments have been made, some of which might be considered actionable. In gathering feedback of this kind, therefore, thought must always be given to the question: what are we going to do with it? It certainly would be unwise to challenge some of these apparent culprits outright, based on the accusations of one (possibly disgruntled) person. The most we can do is to take this sort of comment as evidence that the mentoring relationship isn't working properly – whatever the cause – and investigate further, employing professional tact and discretion. The retention of such feedback in writing is also unwise; and thought must therefore be given to how such confidential, written feedback should be disposed of. An important point to take from this is an ethical one: that, in eliciting written feedback of any kind, care should be taken to discourage the use of names, and to employ a system of numerical or alphabetical tagging which enables you – but no one else – as evaluator or monitor to identify those involved.

What interventions might you want to make?

At this point you might want to arrange meetings with Jo and Lenny and, most urgently, Gill and Lynette. You'll probably be considering replacing Gill and Lynette if your conversations with them are less than reassuring (and this, of course, is assuming you'll manage to tie them down to a meeting). You may also feel it's a good idea to speak with each of their mentees too, to answer their questions and give reassurance where it's needed. Almost certainly you'll want to make an urgent intervention in the case of Parveen, in order to rescue her from what appears to be an inappropriate and largely unsupervised workload.

What other methods of evaluation could have been introduced here?

A more structured questionnaire would have allowed you to set the exact agenda in terms of the questions you wanted answers to. You could have asked, for example, about the frequency, length and content of meetings between mentor and mentee. You could have ascertained whether the mentors had read the Mentor Handbook and how useful they had found it. You could even have asked mentors and mentees about their understanding and expectations of mentoring, as well as their experience of it. On the other hand, a closely structured questionnaire might not have allowed for feedback on certain issues. With too prescriptive a set of questions you might never have discovered, for example, that Parveen is providing unpaid cover, or that Gill is too busy furthering her own career to effectively mentor anyone else's.

Besides the questionnaire, other methods of evaluation which might have been useful would include the following.

Interviews

More time-consuming to carry out and to analyse, and therefore less cost-effective than the questionnaire, the interview would however make possible the exploration of individual answers, as well as providing a method of differentiation. (For example, you might want to ask different questions of different mentors/mentees, according to the apparent strengths and/or weaknesses of the mentoring relationship.)

A comparison between learning plans and outcomes

Taking us back to the first point in this chapter, such a comparison enables us to assess the success of the mentoring against specific criteria.

Logs and diaries

If mentors and, more particularly, mentees are required to keep a journal as part of the mentoring arrangement, these can provide valuable evidence of what is happening in relation to the mentoring arrangement (as we've seen in several of the case studies in earlier chapters).

Group discussion

Group discussion, or focus groups of mentors and/or mentees can be used to identify key issues.

Statistical analysis

A quantitative method such as this can be particularly useful when evaluating on a large scale, with an eye to organisational benefits, but of limited validity when dealing with small numbers of mentoring relationships. Statistics for scrutiny might include those relating to drop-out rates for mentors or mentees; successful completions or promotions; complaints; positive feedback; numbers of mentees becoming mentors themselves; institutional performance indicators such as achievement and retention, and so on.

If you followed up this initial feedback with a questionnaire, what questions would you want to ask?

Your response to the previous question will have gone a long way towards answering this one. An additional question you could ask the mentors might be about what sort of support or professional development they would find useful in helping them with their mentoring role. And to avoid missing any vital feedback (see above) you would probably add an open question, such as what other information or feedback about the mentoring process do you think it would be useful for us to have at this stage?

In reviewing the mentoring programme, what changes might you want to make for the following year?

There are all sorts of ideas you may have come up with here, from reviewing the criteria and operational detail for the selection, recruitment and training of mentors to instigating a system of monitoring which gives effective feedback from the outset of the programme. From the feedback we've just been looking at it would appear that if there is already a system of mentor support in place it certainly needs reviewing in order to improve its effectiveness.

If you were to follow up this monitoring exercise by putting together a development programme for mentors, what would you put on the agenda?

In the first instance you would want to make sure that the issues you picked up from the evaluation were carefully addressed so as to avoid the same problems recurring. Your agenda, then, might look something like this.

a) Clear guidelines about the parameters and purpose of the student teacher's college experience. (Lenny: *She's filling in for one of our team who's off sick and she's managing nearly a full teaching timetable.* And Raj: *What's the maximum number of hours she should be teaching per week?*)

b) Clear guidelines about the mentor's role and what is expected in terms of commitment and time. (Ollie: *I feel like I'm being a nuisance if I try to ask her something. She says to make an appointment to see her, but then she doesn't turn up.* And Jo: *Do I get paid for this?*)

c) The essential skills of mentoring, as set out in the earlier chapters of this book (Pansy: *My mentor has no idea*); and – to follow this up – the further skills of mentoring, including how to give constructive feedback about points for development. (Darren: *She always says everything's fine, though. I'd quite like to know what I could improve on, but my action plan points always come from me.*)

It's clear at once, from the scale of what's to be addressed, that this is not the sort of professional development that can be fitted into one meeting, or even one half-day session. Indeed, the professional development and support of mentors is ideally an ongoing process which proceeds in parallel with the development of the mentee. In this way we support individual mentors and at the same time sustain a system of effective mentoring. The mentoring relationship, when it's working effectively, is a win–win situation, where the mentor can expect to gain just as much as the mentee in terms of his or her professional development. What we should be aiming at is for all the mentors to be saying, along with Raj, *I think I'm learning as much from this as she is!*

CLOSE FOCUS

We have looked here at some of the issues around evaluating a scheme for mentoring student teachers. Imagine now that the scenario we are evaluating changes a little, first to a pilot scheme for mentoring first line managers in leadership skills; and then to a college-wide scheme for mentoring teachers whose appraisal has identified areas for development. Taking each of these scenarios, consider the following questions:

- To what extent will the issues and strategies which we've discussed in this chapter so far remain relevant to these rather different scenarios?
- What additional issues might these new scenarios bring into play?

DISCUSSION

We shall be looking at college-wide issues such as these in some detail in our next and final chapter. In terms of the two questions we've just asked you to think about, your answers are likely to be, first, that all the issues we've raised and the strategies we've discussed in the previous section will apply equally to the two new scenarios. In thinking this through you will probably have made a useful checklist for yourself of what these issues and strategies are, something like this:

- ensure the objective/s of the mentoring are clear to everyone concerned;
- monitor the mentoring arrangement from an early stage;

- elicit formative and summative feedback from the mentor and mentee;
- use a structured (but not over-structured) approach for doing this (e.g. questionnaire);
- use the monitoring and evaluation as a basis from which to review and possibly revise the objectives or operational strategies of the system;
- have clear and realistic criteria for the recruitment and selection of mentors;
- provide mentors with professional development and support.

Secondly, in considering what additional issues these two alternative scenarios might bring into play, you are likely to have come up with factors such as *the purpose* inherent in such evaluations, and the question of what is being evaluated: the extent to which mentoring is meeting individual development needs or institutional needs, or both. You may also have identified some issues relating to quality management. Would you need, for example, to place additional emphasis on the need for sensitivity and tact in mentoring experienced teachers who, despite their proven expertise, may be encountering difficulties with some aspect of their professional practice (classroom management, for example; or supporting the learning of 14–16-year-olds)? And what about logistics? How easily – for a college-wide initiative – would we find sufficient numbers of suitably experienced and qualified teachers and/or leaders who are willing or able to give time to mentoring and how would we ensure quality in our choice, recruitment and monitoring of such mentors? Here again the professional support and development of mentors becomes a key issue, and we can see clearly how the professional development and good practice of its mentors can play a key part in the development and good practice of the college as a whole.

Professional development for the mentor

When we talk about professional development in a mentoring context, we are usually focusing on the mentee. In this chapter, however, we have referred several times to the professional development of the mentor; but what exactly is it, in terms of professional development, that mentors can gain from their role? This is what we're going to look at next.

TASK

1. Think about an experience you have had as mentor. Note down at least two things you can honestly say you gained from the experience. (If you've never yet taken on this role, look back through the earlier chapters of this book and do this exercise from the point of view of one of the effective mentors we've discussed there.)

2. Read through the accounts given by the four mentors below and summarise what they, in their view, have gained from their mentoring experience.

3. How do these two lists compare? Did any of your gains correspond with those of the mentors below?

Mentor A

I think the mentoring is a two-way thing. It has been for me, anyway. When we talk about Dave's teaching it inevitably has me reflecting critically on my own. And even more so when he's been sitting in, observing one of my lessons. He asks stuff like: why did you put them in small groups for that task? Or, why did you tackle the learning objectives in that particular order? Stuff like that. And it makes you think, you know? It makes you more reflective about what you're doing yourself. Because he doesn't miss a trick, our Dave. I don't know what it would be like if I was mentoring some dozy character who didn't know what he was doing. Probably that'd stretch me even more, because I'd have to learn a bit of tact, wouldn't I? Tell him where he's going wrong without getting my nose flattened.

Mentor B

To tell you the truth, I've always thought it would be interesting to work in staff development. When they asked me to be a mentor to newly-appointed staff I thought, Hello! Here's my chance. Here's where I get my foot on the ladder. And actually it's been great. I've put a lot of effort in, mainly because I know exactly what I want out of it. I want the experience and the – you know – status, so I can put it on my cv and say, Look! I've done this. They think enough of me here to ask me to be a mentor. And by agreeing to do it I've demonstrated my commitment to not just my own professional development but professional development in the college as a whole. I know this on its own isn't going to let me walk into a staff development post, but it's a move in the right direction and I'm learning a lot as I go.

Mentor C

I hadn't really thought about my role in terms of leadership skills until I was asked to mentor this new head of section. I hadn't really ever broken it down into this skill and that skill. I just thought I was winging it – making it up as I went along. I suppose I always knew people thought of me as a good head of department, but I hadn't ever sat down and thought through what it was that made them see me that way. So it's been a real steep learning curve for me, this mentoring business. You can't just give out advice: Do it like that because it works for me. If you're giving guidance and helping someone think through the implications of their role – if you're going to do that properly – you have no choice but to look afresh at why and how you do what you do; to start theorising, in other words. Sounds a bit grand, but that, in effect is what it gets you doing. I can articulate now what it is I do that works, and why. I don't just put it down any more to the fact that I'm a nice person or I'm well-organised. There is a method to what I do, and acting as mentor has helped me to discover it and improve on it.

Mentor D

The woman I've been mentoring, she's doing her PGCE at the local uni. And I'll tell you what: she may be completely new to teaching, but she's bang up to date with all the White Papers and consultation documents and policy initiatives and all of that. It's part of the course; and, I mean, normally I'd say I don't have time for all that stuff. I'm working flat out just to get the teaching and marking and that done. Normally I'd wait for somebody to give me a potted version, or I'd catch it in the paper on a Sunday. That's the only way I'd keep up to date. But she's been an eye-opener, has Cheryl. She gives me the website addresses and all that. And it keeps me on my toes. It certainly does. I have to know what's going on, because she wants to discuss it. So the outcome of all this is, I'm the guru now on the latest White Paper; and last week I ended up doing a presentation to the senior curriculum team on the implications of the White Paper for our 14–19 provision. How about that, then?

DISCUSSION

In summary what these mentors, collectively, have gained, are gaining, or could gain in terms of professional development is:

- the encouragement and opportunity to reflect on their own practice (Mentor A: *It makes you more reflective about what you're doing yourself*);
- the skills associated with effective mentoring, such as being able to give difficult feedback (Mentor A: *I'd have to learn a bit of tact, wouldn't I?*);
- enhanced confidence and self-esteem (Mentor B: *They think enough of me here to ask me to be a mentor*);
- opportunities for career development (Mentor B: *Here's where I get my foot on the ladder*);
- the encouragement to analyse, reflect and theorise about their role (Mentor C: *to look afresh at why and how you do what you do; to start theorising*);
- the motivation and opportunity to update own knowledge and skills (Mentor D: *I'm the guru now on the latest White Paper*);
- opportunities for gaining recognition and expanding current role (Mentor D: *doing a presentation to the senior curriculum team on the implications of the White Paper for our 14–19 provision*).

Of course these are not the only ways in which the mentoring role can serve the mentor's own professional development. How did your own list compare? Did you identify gains that we haven't listed here?

Effective mentor = effective teacher

Mentoring is not simply a leadership or supervisory role; the qualities and skills involved are consistent with the qualities and skills implicit in what we think of as 'good teaching' or 'the effective support of learning'.

Moreover, during the earlier chapters we explored the links between mentoring and other aspects of our professional role as educators, such as coaching, teaching, counselling and the pastoral or care taking aspect. We've shown how the boundaries between these roles can be blurred and the skills involved sometimes interchangeable. In this chapter, which focuses on evaluation, we've shown that we need to evaluate our mentoring for exactly the same reason that we need to evaluate our teaching; that is, to discover whether it is working. So this is a good place to summarise exactly how those skills that we might be monitoring and evaluating in our mentors can also be reflected in good classroom practice.

Let's remind ourselves of the essential skills and qualities, as we've defined them so far.

- A desire to help others develop their potential (Chapter Two).
- A desire to learn and grow continuously yourself (Chapter Two).
- An open mind which can suspend judgement of others (Chapter Two).
- A wish to give something back (Chapter Two).
- The ability to build rapport (Chapter Three).
- Listening skills and questioning skills (Chapter Three).
- The skill of reflecting back what someone has said in order to clarify it (Chapter Three).
- The ability to summarise for someone what they have said (Chapter Three).
- The willingness to challenge lazy or negative thinking (Chapter Four).
- The ability to reframe a problem for someone so that they can see it afresh and understand it better (Chapter Four).
- The ability to 'walk a tightrope' between helping too much and too little, between encouraging someone and being honest if they get something wrong.
- The ability to give constructive feedback (Chapter Five).

It is clear from even the most cursory glance that this list of qualities and skills could just as easily be describing the ideal teacher, the expert classroom practitioner that we all aspire to be. In undertaking professional development as mentors, therefore, we are contributing to the development of the college or organisation as a whole, by raising the level of skills and expertise which are transferable right across the spectrum of professional activity, from straightforward classroom teaching to whole-college staff development.

The learning organisation

Imagine an organisation in which everyone is committed to their own continuing learning and development; in which the skills and qualities we've just listed above are prized and encouraged across the board, from the learning support assistant on a fractional contract to the principal and chair of governors; where everyone is working towards an agreed purpose, which – however it is dressed up in the mission statement – is basically about supporting and encouraging learning. This is what we mean when we talk about a *Learning Organisation*. The *Learning Organisation* is a term used to describe an organisation in which people, whatever their level of status or seniority, are, as individuals or as teams, continually working to increase their effectiveness to produce outcomes about which they really care.

If you look up *Learning Organisation* on the internet you will find a huge range of sites. One thing they all have in common, however, is their definition of this term. In every case it denotes an organisation which, because its personnel are themselves committed to learning, can cope with constant demands for change; an organisation where there is a determination to change things for the better, to go on improving; and one which makes room for creative ideas and risk-taking. Above all, it is an organisation which doesn't at any point draw a line under anyone's learning or development and say, okay, that's it, you can stop learning now. And neither does it become complacent about its own organisational development and learning. Mentoring and the effective evaluation of mentoring is integral to the way that we develop this kind of culture. It is indicative of a college or institution that values not just learning, and not just learning to learn, but promotes an ethos of learning to learn how to learn. To demonstrate what we mean by this, we can express it as a series of steps like this:

Mentoring and organisational learning

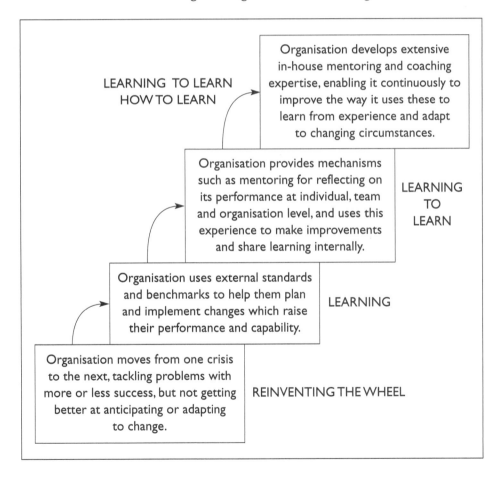

This diagram is designed to demonstrate that, although *individual* professional development is central to the mentoring relationship, mentoring should also be seen very clearly as *central to the development of the college as a whole*, in terms both of reflecting and of driving its institutional attitudes to learning and change. We shall have more to say about whole-college issues in the next chapter. Meanwhile, as the final section of this chapter has stressed, effective and robustly monitored mentoring – as well as excellent teaching – is part of what turns a college into a learning organisation.

Summary

In this chapter we have looked at some of the issues relating to why and how we might evaluate mentoring on an individual relationship level, a programme level and an institutional level. We have seen that monitoring and evaluation are ongoing processes which might be approached in a number of ways. We have also looked at how such monitoring and evaluation is an essential part of institutional quality assurance, contributing towards the development and promotion of learning throughout the organisation. In the next chapter we shall turn our attention to the organisation itself.

Further reading

Cunningham, B (2004) Some have mentoring thrust upon them: the element of choice in mentoring in a PCET environment. *Research in Post-Compulsory Education*, 9, 2, pp 271–282.

Hankey, J (2004) The good, the bad and other considerations: reflections on mentoring trainee teachers in post-compulsory education. *Research in Post-Compulsory Education*, 9, 3, pp 389–400.

Woodd, M (2001) Learning to leap from a peer: a research study on mentoring in a further and higher education institution. *Research in Post-Compulsory Education*, 6, 1, pp 97–104.

There are some interesting websites which explore issues around setting up, monitoring and evaluating mentoring schemes. For example:
www.nfie.org/publications/mentoring.htm;
www.peer.ca/mentor.html.

Mentoring schemes – institutional issues

CHAPTER OBJECTIVES

This chapter is designed to help you to:

identify factors which may impact on the success of mentoring in your college;

identify some of the possible objectives of mentoring schemes;

- identify ways of assessing the readiness of the organisation for institution-wide mentoring schemes;

- explore ways in which mentoring can be integrated with other development activity;

- identify some of the important questions which an institution may need to ask itself when implementing a mentoring scheme;

- consider some of the institutional and organisational issues involved in training mentors and mentees.

Introduction

Most of this book has concentrated on useful information for FE staff finding themselves in the role of mentor or mentee; but what of the implications for the college in which the mentoring takes place? The institution frequently plays a role in organising and managing the provision of mentoring, and there are a number of issues for colleges to bear in mind when addressing this task.

This chapter, therefore, is aimed more at those poor souls responsible for running the mentoring scheme in a college and the management teams who delegated this job to them with such obvious sighs of relief. We examine what factors may impact on the success of mentoring in your college. We discuss some of the possible objectives of mentoring, the importance of gauging the readiness of the organisation for such approaches and the integration of mentoring with other development activity. Assuming it is agreed to implement some kind of formal mentoring scheme, decisions need to be made about what the characteristics of this might be and we also look at some of the pros and cons of these decisions in this chapter. We do not have the space here to rehearse all of the arguments for and against various approaches, but we try to cover most of the important questions which an institution may need to ask itself when implementing a mentoring scheme. Finally, we touch upon some of the considerations involved in training mentors and mentees, and how some of the risks inherent in introducing mentoring may be avoided.

What are your objectives?

As with any aspect of policy or strategy, it is essential to be clear about what it is you are trying to achieve. At first sight this may seem obvious. The purpose of mentoring from the organisation's point of view is to develop teachers, and maybe to help the college meet national targets and standards in this area.

Professional development

Even if we limit ourselves to these important objectives, it may be helpful to unpick them a little further. Is the objective of mentoring merely to help trainee and newly-qualified teachers, or do we see it as a more fundamental building block of continuing professional development for staff at all levels? More experienced and senior staff can potentially benefit from the experience of being mentored just as much as new teachers. As a busy lecturer in an FE college, for example, how many opportunities exist currently to interact and share experiences with your professional peer group? Spending all your time with students provides plenty of opportunity to practise your skills, but precious little perhaps to reflect on them and learn from your experience. Furthermore, those acting as mentors will themselves undoubtedly derive some professional benefit from using and improving their mentoring and coaching skills on a day-to-day basis. As we saw in Chapter Seven, coaching and mentoring can help further develop key skills used in teaching. So does the college aim to use mentoring as a means to develop teaching skills at all levels?

Maybe part of the college's plan is to encourage individuals to take greater responsibility for their own development. The concept of 'self-managed learning' will not be a new one to many readers. You may have dealings with companies who are themselves trying to position continuing development as a matter of individual initiative, rather than something which employees have 'done to them'. Whether this is prompted by a growing trend towards individual autonomy in the workplace or by the gradual reduction of large, well-staffed training departments and a squeeze on budgets depends on your point of view.

It may be, though, that there is a financial agenda at work here, as far as the college is concerned. Depending on how mentoring is resourced and rewarded, it is quite possible to argue that mentoring is a less costly form of professional development than many alternatives, such as in-service training courses, or professional conferences and seminars. It may be seen as constituting better value for money than some other development options, as we discussed in Chapter One. We know that organisations outside the educational sector have been attracted to coaching and mentoring as an alternative to formal courses for reasons of both efficacy *and* cost. Training and development budgets come under pressure in most organisations, at some time or another. It pays us to acknowledge whether this is a factor in our own decision to introduce mentoring, because it may affect decisions about the design and structure of the scheme.

Other objectives

So there are a number of things to consider, even within the apparently simple objective of developing teachers. But what if we look beyond this agenda to other potential reasons for introducing more mentoring into the Lifelong Learning sector?

There is an obvious connection between development and performance, and yet we have so far ignored performance assessment/performance improvement as a possible objective for introducing mentoring. Still a relatively new and sensitive issue within education, performance management will, nonetheless, continue to be a feature of the professional teacher's career in future, and it may be that mentoring is designed to be an integral part of this. The one-to-one attention offered by mentoring, and its emphasis on taking charge of one's own development, can be enormously motivating. But that is not all. Regular, less formal conversations, geared to continuing development and mutual learning, may offer a useful addition, or even an antidote, to traditional models of organisation-wide annual appraisal. And what of future potential and career planning? Whatever mechanisms may exist in colleges at the present time to identify future potential and to develop talent for growth and succession, it is not hard to see how mentoring might be an integral part of this strategy.

As colleges compete to attract and hold on to the best staff, the benefits of motivating and retaining good teachers rises up the management agenda. It would be naïve to assume that factors such as salary, promotion, location and a host of others did not play a part in such decisions, but there is plenty of evidence to suggest that feeling valued and being supported in one's professional development are equally important factors in people's decision to stay with an employer or look elsewhere.

Finally, we should not overlook the capacity for mentoring to broaden an individual's horizons in areas other than just their professional practice. Other aspects of the organisation's culture may benefit from the challenge to existing preconceptions which mentoring can provide. Diversity policies, for example, may be well served by a process which exposes staff to perspectives from across the age, gender or ethnic divide.

In this brief section we have explored some of the objectives which the institution may care to consider when developing its approach to using mentoring. Hopefully, in the process, we have broadened out the possible agenda from a straightforward teacher training issue to much more universal questions of staff development, organisational performance and the college's competitiveness as both employer and educational provider. Why is the identification of objectives important? Because unless we are clear about this, we will find it difficult to make other decisions.

- How will the effectiveness of mentoring be evaluated (Chapter Seven)?
- How should we position the mentoring internally (see below)?

- What should the training consist of for mentors and/or mentees?
- What is the cost of our investment in mentoring?
- What sort of payback are we getting on our investment?

Clear objectives are important for mentors and learners, because they create focus and enable them to see how far they have come. In the same way, without clear, preferably measurable, objectives at the institutional level we will find it impossible to determine how useful a mentoring programme has been.

Is the organisation ready for mentoring?

In one sense mentoring may be viewed as simply a technique for staff development, like any other. But at the organisational level it brings with it a number of cultural dimensions which may have a dramatic effect on its likelihood of success. What signs should we look for to tell us how ready a college might be for the introduction of mentoring?

To what extent does your institution value continuous learning and development? It may appear a facetious question to ask an organisation in the Lifelong Learning sector, but the reality is that staff development is conditional upon existing staff profile, budgets, management style and institutional strategy, all of which may vary from place to place. Do all your staff, from the newest teacher to the principal, embrace the idea that they never stop learning? Would they welcome the opportunity to reflect on their professional practice (after 15 or 20 years' experience maybe) and map out areas for development? How might they respond to the suggestion that they should undertake mentor training, or be allocated a mentor themselves? Yes, well, perhaps our initial question is not so facetious after all.

No organisation can be immune to the sensitivities surrounding individuals' competence and performance. How staff respond to such questions will depend on both their own values and beliefs and the culture that the college tries to promote. For example, an institution afraid of insulting its experienced teaching staff by suggesting they need training in mentoring may wish to reflect further on its commitment to continuous learning and development.

When addressing matters of institutional culture, a good place to start is at the top. It is said that an organisation's culture is partly a shadow of its leaders. So, does the management style of the organisation reflect a strong desire to control activities and outcomes, or a belief in individual autonomy and delegation of authority to the lowest possible level? As we have already said, mentoring relies on a more self-managed approach to learning and development. It assumes people will make mistakes, but then derive their own learning from the experience. It is hard to see it operating in quite this way in an environment where staff are expected to do as they are told and avoid rocking the boat or questioning the status quo.

What if the organisation sees mentoring as part of its strategy to *change* the culture? It is true that mentoring and coaching can play a key role in helping individuals to change, as we have seen already and, by extension, we can see how this might translate into wider cultural change. But this does depend on who does the mentoring and how much control over this the organisation feels able to exercise. It is worth remembering that mentoring can be as much a force for maintaining the status quo as for generating change.

Do you have senior management commitment to the introduction of mentoring? Other than asking them and watching them nod sagely in agreement (not a cast-iron guarantee, in our humble opinion), what can you do to assess this commitment? Here are some thoughts.

- Do they embrace the idea of continuous learning?
- How is *their* performance reviewed? Do *they* have development plans?
- Have they experience of being mentored or coached in the past?
- Are they undergoing mentoring or coaching currently?
- Are they willing to be trained as mentors?
- Do they try to adopt a mentoring/coaching approach when leading their own teams?

Remember that right at the beginning of this book we talked about mentoring being more than a series of techniques or a skills toolkit. It is a way of behaving, a habit if you will, and the greatest difficulty in introducing it successfully to an organisation is not so much learning the skills as getting the habit. What are the chances, do you think, of the organisation getting the habit if the most senior managers do not?

The readiness of the institution may also be affected by its previous experience of mentoring. It may already be well established in parts of the college and working well. On the other hand it may have been poorly introduced or experimented with in the past, and now be marked out as a 'failed initiative'. This will make it harder to get mentors and mentees excited about the prospect of its more widespread use. Furthermore, those colleges which have already had some positive experience of mentoring are likely to have developed key skills amongst some of their staff already.

Finally, readiness may be a function of how well mentoring is integrated into the wider people strategy of the college. We touched on this when we looked at possible institutional objectives earlier. One could see how mentoring may be an important element, for example, of a college's strategy for gaining Investors in People status. At the very least, questions such as how formal or informal the scheme should be, and how learner-driven, will be determined in large part by the institution's overall approach to people management. We go on to explore some of these choices further below.

So the readiness of the college to embrace mentoring successfully as a development or performance improvement strategy will be affected by a number of factors, including:

- culture of the organisation;
- management style;
- previous experience;
- overall people strategy.

Those responsible for introducing or managing a formal mentoring scheme within an institution need to assess the likely hurdles and sources of resistance by using the headings above to ask themselves how ready the organisation is for mentoring, and how the introduction may be handled in order to maximise its chances of success.

Does mentoring fit well with other development activity?

Integration of mentoring with a broader people strategy is one measure of the college's readiness, and research suggests that mentoring has worked better in organisations where it is a part of that overall strategy than where it is a bolt-on. At a more detailed level, this is also true of the 'fit' between mentoring and other development activity. Is it an integral part of continuing professional development policies in your college? Do you make use of particular competency standards and, if so, are mentors trained and encouraged to use these appropriately in coaching? What role does mentoring play, if any, in succession planning, leadership development, or performance management? The answers to these questions may inform key choices about the nature of your mentoring programme.

TASK

Before we go on to look at some of these choices, let us pause here to reflect on some of the issues raised so far. Read through the brief case study below and see if you can identify some of the factors which will potentially assist the introduction of mentoring into Crawford College and the likely obstacles that will have to be overcome.

Crawford College, a medium-sized college of FE in a large city, is one of several FE institutions serving the conurbation. It has recently appointed a new principal, Sarah Barker, who has made a reputation turning round a poorly performing college in Inner London. She is determined to raise the profile and reputation of Crawford College in the city, as she foresees rationalisation amongst the colleges competing for students as pretty inevitable, and is keen for Crawford to be a major player in this, rather than a victim of it.

The senior team which she has inherited is a mix of new blood and long-established staff. In particular one of the vice-principals, Jim Speddings, seems to be very influential, having worked at the college for over 20 years and acted as principal, in a caretaking capacity, immediately before the latest appointment. But Jim, like a number of his senior colleagues, is due to retire within the next five years and no obvious successors seem to have been identified internally.

Sarah's staff development officer, Mel, has some good ideas about how they might introduce new standards and competencies, but has been keeping her head down since a disastrous pilot for an in-house coaching scheme 12 months or so ago. It had been trialled in Jim Speddings's school, and never really overcame Jim's initial cynicism about the whole initiative. What professional development does take place currently is largely as a result of Mel spotting a likely-looking conference or seminar and suggesting it to an appropriate member of staff. Sarah has already talked to her about a more multi-method approach to training and development.

The previous principal had, by all accounts, been well respected, though largely for the way he took a tough line over expenditure as rolls fell year on year. He ruled senior staff meetings with a rod of iron, but was seen as a 'safe pair of hands'. While Sarah has a reputation for not suffering fools gladly, she has a more 'hands-off' approach and expects her team to take full responsibility for delivering on their own parts of the strategy. To support this she is introducing clear, measurable performance targets for her own team and has already carried out an appraisal with each one. A previous boss of hers, now retired, has been a great influence on her and she still keeps in regular touch. She is very open about how he saw her through some of the darkest hours of her previous job.

What factors did you identify? What more might you want to know? What other questions would you want answered?

Features of mentoring schemes – what is appropriate to your environment?

Formal vs informal

In much of what we have said so far we have tended to assume that the organisation is actively sponsoring and managing the mentoring activity, but this may not be the case. Informal mentoring is often seen as more successful, because mentees tend to select their own mentors, the relationship often growing out of some other association, rather like Sarah Barker and her old boss. This usually means that the 'chemistry' is there already and one of the causes of failed partnerships is avoided. It is nothing new for less experienced teachers to go to staff they admire and get on well with, and ask them for help and advice. It is unlikely that formal allocation of mentors to mentees by a scheme organiser will achieve as high a compatibility rate as free choice by mentees.

The problem, of course, is informal approaches do not ensure that everyone who needs a mentor gets one. Nor do they allow for monitoring or evaluation. You may require some basic record-keeping of mentoring sessions, balancing confidentiality with the need for continuous improvement of the process. In an entirely informal setting no one is accountable for the overall success or failure of mentoring, and there is no institutional provision to set time and resources aside for this important activity. And what of contracting? Can the college be satisfied that confidentiality and other ethical considerations are being properly observed, if there is no overall coordination? There may be a fear that, left to their own devices, mentees might choose mentors who are somehow 'unsuitable'. Being mentored by a friendly colleague every Friday evening down the pub may be great fun, but less than convincing as a basis for CPD. There is nothing to say that mentoring must be entirely formal or entirely informal, of course, but the college will need to decide if it wishes to encourage both sorts of mentoring. Assuming that some degree of formality is chosen, a number of other choices follow.

Voluntary vs compulsory

Is mentoring a compulsory element of your staff development programmes, or do people have a choice as to whether they are mentored? Perhaps this varies according to different categories of staff, so trainee and newly-qualified teachers are allocated mentors as a matter of course, but more experienced teachers may choose. Whatever the circumstances, who is responsible for managing the relationship? Are mentees expected to draw on help from their mentor or is it up to mentors to ensure that the appropriate progress is being made? Research would seem to suggest that compulsory mentoring has a higher failure rate, mainly because successful mentoring relies on the mentee *wanting* the help. Those who have mentoring thrust upon them are less likely to get the full benefit from the process.

How much control of matching?

We know from previous chapters that compatibility plays a major role in the success or failure of mentoring relationships. What can the organisation do to maximise the chances of success? Arguably, they could just back off. It is possible to have a formal scheme which puts the onus on the mentee to find an appropriate mentor. However, for a newly-appointed teacher or a trainee this would be a difficult task, with no guarantee of a positive outcome. What happens, for example, if their choice is not a trained mentor? You may understandably feel that some control of matching is preferable, if only for certain groups.

The first task the college must address is the selection and training of 'suitable' mentors, itself a potentially sensitive undertaking. Chapter Two will help you to determine desirable qualities and therefore selection criteria. Chapters Three, Four and Five will help with training content and later in this chapter we will be looking at different approaches to training. But, having identified and trained your pool of mentors, do you allow mentees some choice, take pot luck, or structure a process for matching mentor and mentee according to some set of agreed criteria? You may decide to select a shortlist of suitable mentors, against certain criteria, but then allow the mentee some choice to account for personal chemistry. Maybe speed dating provides an attractive model. (It never provided me with one.) Mentees could be encouraged to meet informally with a number of mentors at a prearranged event, and preferences expressed via the scheme organiser, in order to avoid bitter memories of playground team selection. What provision is there if a relationship fails to work?

If the decision is to provide matching as an organisation, there are some factors you may wish to consider in brokering these relationships (remember these are areas where mentees may have some preference, it is not necessarily desirable to match people with someone just like them):

- department or discipline within the college;
- position in the staff hierarchy;
- age/experience;
- learning style;
- personality;
- gender;
- ethnicity.

Role of the mentor

We have seen already what a broad variety of functions a mentor can fulfil. As an institution you may wish to circumscribe this in some way, or even identify different types of mentor, on the grounds that not everyone is willing or able to undertake the full range of roles. You may choose to have 'buddy' mentors, people who concentrate on assisting staff new to the college, subject specialists, people who only help with the professional development of teachers in their own department, or maybe separate 'career development' mentors to help people formulate longer-term plans for their professional development. (There are some suggestions for further reading on this topic and others at the end of this chapter.)

Despite the difficulties inherent in defining mentoring, the college may wish to provide guidance internally as to where it sees the mentor's role beginning and ending, if only in the interests of protecting both parties. Chapter Two gives you some useful guidance on what the role may or may not include.

How to position the mentoring with college staff

We have mentioned the importance of objectives already, and clarity of purpose is certainly an advantage when presenting the idea of mentoring within the college. Who is eligible for mentoring and why? What are the expected payoffs for the individuals involved and the college? Will it be perceived as excluding any group and how might this be explained? Is it primarily a 'line' function, that is to say something your immediate manager does, or is it deliberately positioned outside of the managerial relationship? Is it promoted as a two-way process with mutual learning benefits for mentee and mentor, or simply a support service to less experienced staff? The answers to these questions, along with others already suggested, may determine whether mentoring gets seen as an exciting new source of development available to staff if they want it, or another means of checking up on people's performance, or even, at worst, a remedial measure for inexperienced and failing teachers, who need someone else to help them do their job properly.

How to approach the introduction of mentoring

At one extreme an organisation may decide to introduce mentoring wholesale across all relevant staff at one go. This has advantages in terms of equality of opportunity, but is a daunting task, and leaves less scope for learning from one's mistakes. An alternative would be to pilot mentoring with one group or in one school/faculty and grow the scheme gradually from there. This allows for evaluation and learning along the way, and gives more time for getting everyone on board with the benefits of the process. Thought could be given to looking at existing networks within the college to see whether advantage can be taken of these to integrate mentoring better into the fabric of the organisation.

What sort of training to do

The first decision here is whether to provide any formal training at all for staff taking part in mentoring. As we have already indicated, you may meet some resistance to the idea of professional educators receiving training in what they see as essentially teaching and coaching skills. However, past experience would suggest that training helps enormously in establishing boundaries, setting expectations, alerting participants to ethical issues and generally ensuring that relationships get off to a productive start. It is also highly unusual, in our view, for people not to develop some new skills, however experienced they may consider themselves to be in related areas. What is more, the people who will make the greatest success of being a mentor or a mentee are likely to be those most anxious to undertake training.

So should training be provided for mentors only, mentees only, or mentors and mentees; and, if both, should they be trained separately or together? Ultimately this may be driven partly by practical considerations of availability, group size and scheme design. It may also be affected by the culture of the organisation. The problem with training mentors only is that one half of the relationship remains more ignorant of its purpose, scope and dynamics. Not only are mentees less likely to get the full benefit as quickly, but, importantly, they are put at a disadvantage. Institutions must remain alert to the impact of power and politics on mentoring relationships and the dangers inherent in either party abusing their power. We touched on this in Chapter Four when we examined some of the ethical issues in mentoring. Whatever the organisational status differences between mentor and mentee, the best relationships seem to work on the basis of equality, creating an environment free of political baggage and therefore more conducive to mutual trust and learning.

Training mentees only is an interesting approach, emphasising the responsibility of the learner for her own development, and creating a degree of demand for mentoring, rather than it being something which is done *to* the learner. Whilst giving the mentee more responsibility and authority, however, it does not address the problem of mentor quality and the dangers of toxic mentoring, which we have alluded to in earlier chapters.

Schemes have been successful using a variety of different approaches to training, so we will avoid being too prescriptive here. There are, nevertheless, a number of features, which we would suggest scheme organisers at least give careful thought to.

- Providing some training to both mentors and mentees, although the balance might depend on how much the college wishes to emphasise the mentee's responsibility for the relationship.

- Involving joint mentor/mentee groups in at least some of the training, if possible. Amongst other advantages this helps to create an openness about the nature of the relationship, which may prevent it becoming an awkward or taboo topic of discussion later on.

- Using a mix of training approaches, rather than just classroom briefings and role play. Mentors can learn a lot from both practice and being mentored themselves. Therefore a reflective journal, as described in Chapter Six, combined with some mentoring for the mentors, or perhaps learning group sessions to share experience, would go a long way towards embedding the practices studied in the classroom.

Supervision

This brings us neatly to the idea of supervision. There are a number of reasons why an organisation may want to consider establishing some suitably confidential system of supervision, or mentoring for the mentors.

- *Continuing professional development.* If we are serious about lifelong learning, then mentoring, like any other skill, is something we can continue to get better at.

- *Preventing undue stress on the care taker.* We have seen how mentoring involves more than just professional development and support. It frequently requires the mentor to lend an empathetic ear to other, more personal issues. Just as in other care taking situations, if the mentor has no outlet for expressing their own emotional response to this it may, over time, have a damaging effect on their wellbeing.

- *Ensuring healthy relationships and ethical standards.* A forum in which mentors can discuss difficult aspects of their mentoring relationships will help to avert or resolve ethical dilemmas and avoid potentially damaging and manipulative behaviour.

This supervision may be provided in a number of different ways, including these.

- Externally, via experienced mentors from outside the college.
- Internally, via peer mentoring, encouraging mentors to 'buddy' each other in order to provide mutual supervision.
- Internally, via a small team of more experienced 'master mentors', who are responsible for quality assurance and development of the mentoring scheme.

The idea of peer mentoring, of course, can be extended beyond the confines of formal supervision. The college may see wider benefits in the idea of heads of school, for example, mentoring each other, to share experience and best practice. It is not difficult to imagine the political barriers that such an initiative may come up against, but the benefits of confronting these may be significant. As more FE teachers complete pre-service and in-service training earlier on in their careers, there may be an increasing value in peer exchanges and mentoring as a way of developing best practice.

TASK

Let us now hear from a mentee. Her name is Heather and she is an experienced, part-time teacher undertaking in-service training. As she describes her impressions of the mentoring scheme in her particular college, try to associate some of the good and bad aspects of the scheme with the features we have outlined in this chapter. Think about what changes you might make to the mentoring programme in Heather's college to make it more effective.

My mentor's name is Bruno. He's a lovely bloke. Always makes time for me and tries to help, but we've never really clicked. I'm never one to keep my opinions to myself and love a good laugh, whereas Bruno's a bit quiet and serious. Also his background and the way he came into teaching are so different from me. Still, there wasn't anyone else available, so I suppose we're stuck with each other!

I shouldn't complain. It's not too bad now we've sorted what we're about. The first two or three meetings were a bit confusing for me, as I wasn't quite sure what sort of help to expect. In fact I was a bit worried, to tell the truth, as to why I'd been given a mentor at all. I thought I'd been doing pretty well in all the assignments and classroom observations, but the only people who seem to have had a mentor in the past have been those who got a bit hammered by the inspectors in their last report. So I guess I was a bit distrustful of poor old Bruno at first.

Still now, as I say, things are okay. Bruno got some really helpful guidelines on the mentor's role during his training, so he could help me think about what I might get out of it. And it's good to be able to speak openly to someone who's not my boss, or even in my department. As a part-timer for many years, I suppose I felt a bit more isolated than most, so it wouldn't have been easy to get a mentor without the college's help, and now I feel I at least have someone to talk to about any worries or difficulties I'm having with the job. I'm careful, though, about how much I unload on Bruno, partly because we don't quite have that sort of rapport, but also because I can see how much pressure he's under. The mentoring here seems to operate pretty much on goodwill, so I'm probably quite lucky that Bruno is as conscientious about meetings and stuff as he is. Some of the other mentors set a terrible example as far as that's concerned. They seem to think they can mess people about as much as they like because they're more senior and their mentees are trainees.

DISCUSSION

You will no doubt have recognised that matching seems a bit haphazard, and there is little that mentors or mentees feel able to do about it. Heather does not appear to have had much training, or much idea what Bruno's role was, though thankfully Bruno's training seemed to have equipped him to put this right. The way the scheme has been introduced seems to have created the impression that mentoring is some sort of remedial activity, and there is little support for Bruno in his mentoring role by way of resources or supervision. Having said this, Heather feels she benefits from the off-line help that Bruno provides. Evaluation and monitoring appear to be non-existent. What changes would you make?

Risks of formal mentoring schemes

In reviewing some of the choices institutions must make when introducing formal mentoring schemes, we have hopefully highlighted some of the risks inherent in any organisational mentoring programme. Here is a reminder of some of them.

- *Time demands.* Without support and resources mentoring is a hard habit to keep up.
- *Poor mentors/poor mentees.* People need help to get the most from the process. This is about selection, matching and training.
- *Cloning and reinforcing poor practice.* The quality of your mentors will affect the quality of your new and existing teachers. This is about selection and training.
- *Unclear expectations.* Nothing will kill a mentoring partnership quicker than people not knowing what they are there for. Once again, training is paramount.
- *Poor personal chemistry.* Hard to cater for, but one of the biggest factors in success or failure. Matching processes need to accommodate it.
- *Demotivation of mentees.* Often the result of any of the above, but also brought on by mentoring schemes positioned as remedial, there to 'knock the learner into shape'.
- *Compulsion.* Mentoring by force is a thankless and ultimately fruitless activity. Try allowing some self-determination and choice in your scheme.
- *Drift.* Without some sort of evaluation and reporting you may find your scheme stagnating or turning toxic. Can you provide quality assurance and support without sacrificing confidentiality and autonomy?

Here is a diagram which summarises the main success factors for a mentoring scheme, and the areas we need to address in order to meet these.

Mentoring success factors

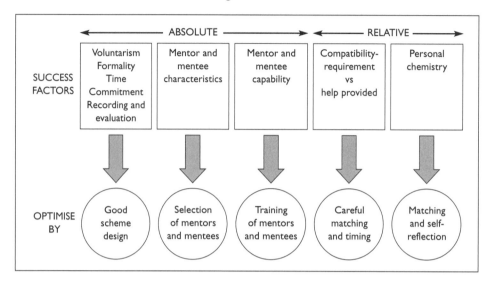

Absolute factors are those for which clear standards can be agreed and decisions made. Relative factors, on the other hand, depend on the way the mentor and mentee relate to each other and highlight, therefore, the importance of matching.

Summary

In this chapter we have examined three areas which might affect a college's approach to making more use of mentoring in its staff development.

- Objectives for introducing mentoring in the first place.
- Readiness of the organisation for mentoring.
- Fit between mentoring and other development activity.

We have discussed some of the pros and cons of formal and informal approaches and gone on to outline some of the key choices open to organisations in designing a formal mentoring scheme. These cover such issues as:

- voluntarism;
- matching;
- mentor/mentee roles;
- internal positioning of scheme;
- method of introduction;
- training approaches;
- supervision.

Finally, we have reviewed some of the risks to be guarded against in designing and implementing a mentoring programme and how these might be avoided.

References and further reading

Frost, PJ (2003) *Toxic Emotions at Work*. Boston, MA: Harvard Business School Press.

Klasen, N and Clutterbuck, D (2002) *Implementing Mentoring Schemes – A Practical Guide to Successful Programs*. Oxford: Butterworth Heinemann.

Woodd, M (2001) Learning to leap from a peer: a research study on mentoring in a further and higher education institution. *Research in Post-Compulsory Education*. 6, 1, pp 97–104.

LRC Radbrook